Golf is, in part, a game; but only in part.
It is also in part a religion, a fever, a vice,
a mirage, a frenzy, a fear, an abscess, a joy, a thrill,
a pest, a disease, an uplift, a brooding melancholy,
a dream of yesterday, a disappointing today
and a hope for tomorrow.

Grantland Rice

1,001 Reasons to Love GOLF

Hubert Pedroli & Mary Tiegreen

Stewart, Tabori & Chang
New York

Published in 2003 by
Stewart, Tabori & Chang
A Company of La Martinière Groupe
115 West 18th Street
New York, NY 10011

Export Sales to all countries except Canada, France,
and French-speaking Switzerland:
Thames and Hudson Ltd.
181A High Holborn
London WC1V 7QX
England

Canadian Distribution:
Canadian Manda Group
One Atlantic Avenue, Suite 105
Toronto, Ontario M6K 3E7
Canada

Library of Congress Cataloging-in-Publication Data
Pedroli, Hubert.
1001 reasons to love golf / Hubert Pedroli & Mary Tiegreen.
p. cm.
ISBN 1-58479-311-2
1. Golf. I. Title: 1001 reasons to love golf. II. Title: One thousand and one reasons
to love golf. III. Tiegreen, Mary. IV. Title.
GV965.P393 2003
796.352-dc21
2003054212
Designed by Mary Tiegreen
Printed in China

10 9 8 7 6 5 4 3 2 1
First Printing

Contents

Great Golf Courses

The Natural Beauty of Golf

Memorable Moments
& Inspirational Characters

Champions, Tournaments, Celebrities & Famous Caddies

Golf Stuff

Introduction

Anyone who's ever spent time with a passionate golfer knows that there is something mysteriously appealing about this Royal & Ancient game. We've all seen golfers go from playing with mild interest to being completely obsessed with the game, often after their first really good drive. What is it about golf that captivates us? What makes it, as Bobby Jones called it, "a game of considerable passion?" Much has been written in an attempt to understand this complex sport. Clearly, it is not one thing but a collection of experiences, large and small, that make up the love of golf.

We started a list one evening, just for fun. Being the first group out on a beautiful summer morning. A regular foursome. Finding a new golf ball in the rough. We asked our fellow golfers what it is that they love about the game. (Fortunately, making a golfer talk about golf isn't too difficult.) Friends, relatives, and golfing acquaintances shared their experiences with us as we compiled an ever-growing list. Many spoke of friendships, the beauty of nature, a cold beer at 19th hole, recounting holes and strokes at the end of a round. Golf schools, vacations, and infomercials. The promise of improvement. Playing golf with your son or daughter. Evenings at the driving range. A new driver that adds 10 yards to your tee shot, a beautiful chip to an elevated green, sinking a 20-foot putt.

As the list grew we began to have a picture of this multi-faceted game. If there are 1,001 reasons then there are surely 1,002. Why we love golf is an endless list of personal experiences and cherished memories. And yet, in the end, golf will always be more than we can ever explain.

Hubert Pedroli & Mary Tiegreen

*T*hree things are as unfathomable as they are fascinating to the masculine mind:

metaphysics, golf, and the feminine heart.

The Germans, I believe, pretend to have solved some of the riddles of the first, and the French to have unraveled some of the intricacies of the last; will someone tell us wherein lies

the extraordinary fascination of golf?

Arnold Haultain
The Mystery of Golf

1 Golf presents us with endless mysteries.

2
The first day of golf after a long winter

Happy Anticipation

It was a morning when all nature shouted "Fore!" The breeze, as it blew gently up from the valley, seemed to bring a message of hope and cheer, whispering of chip shots holed and brassies landing squarely on the meat. The fairway, as yet unscarred by the irons of a hundred dubs, smiled greenly up at the azure sky; and the sun, peeping above the trees, looked like a giant golf ball perfectly lofted by the mashie of some unseen god and about to drop dead by the pin of the eighteenth. It was the day of the opening of the course after the long winter, and a crowd of considerable dimensions had collected at the first tee. Plus fours gleamed in the sunshine, and the air was charged with happy anticipation.

P. G. Wodehouse
The Heart of a Goof, 1926

3
An afternoon stolen from work, enjoying the freedom of the links

4
A trusted set of old clubs

5
Sitting in the shade, waiting to tee off

14

7
The solid sound of a balata ball hit with a wooden driver

8
Mulligans

6
Pull carts

9
Watching the previous group hitting their tee shots

15

A round of golf partakes of the journey, and the journey is one of the central myths and signs of Western man ... if it is a journey, it is also a round: it always leads back to the place where you started from.

Michael Murphy
Golf in the Kingdom

11 Playing downwind from an elevated tee

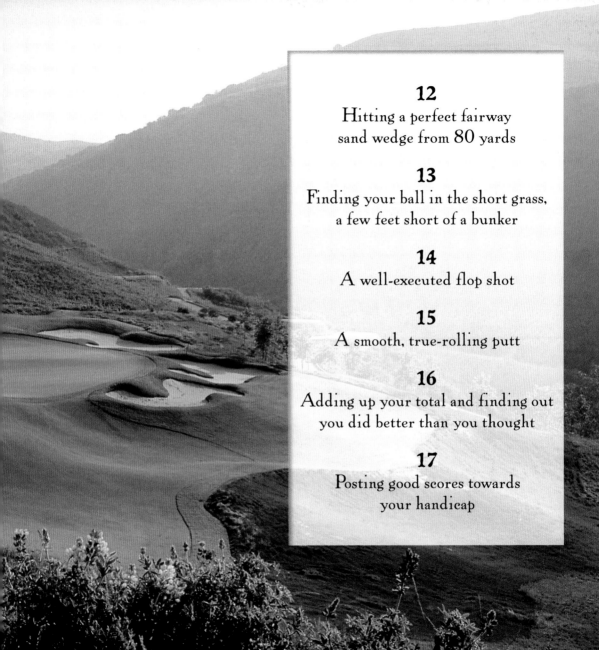

12
Hitting a perfect fairway
sand wedge from 80 yards

13
Finding your ball in the short grass,
a few feet short of a bunker

14
A well-executed flop shot

15
A smooth, true-rolling putt

16
Adding up your total and finding out
you did better than you thought

17
Posting good scores towards
your handicap

The Supreme Joy of Life

I have sometimes heard good golfers sigh regretfully, after holing out on the 18th green, that in the best of circumstances as to health and duration of life they cannot hope for more than another twenty, or thirty, or forty years of golf, and they are then very likely inclined to be a little bitter about the good years of their youth that they may have "wasted" at some other less fascinating sport.

When the golfer's mind turns to reflections such as these, you may depend upon it that it has been one of those days when everything has gone right and nothing wrong, and the supreme joy of life has been experienced on the links. The little white ball has seemed possessed of a soul—a soul full of kindness and the desire for doing good. The clubs have seemed endowed with some subtle qualities that had rarely been discovered in them before. Their lie, their balance, their whip, have appeared to reach the ideal, and such command has been felt over them as over a dissecting instrument in the hands of a skillful surgeon. The sun has been shining and the atmosphere has sparkled when, flicked cleanly from the tee, the rubber-cored ball has been sent singing through the air. The drives have all been long and straight, the brassie shots well up, the approaches mostly dead, and the putts have taken the true line to the tin. Hole after hole has been done in bogey and here and there the common enemy has been beaten by a stroke.

Perhaps the result is a record round, and, so great is the enthusiasm for the game at this moment, that it is regarded as a great misfortune that the sun has set and there is no more light left to play.

Harry Vardon
The Complete Golfer

18

Clearing the water with room to spare

Golf is the foundation of the
most enduring friendships.
The many hours spent together
in our desperate attempts
to break 90 or 100 fosters
strong ties among us.
Or, as some would simply say,
"misery loves company."

Hubert Pedroli

19
A regular Sunday foursome

when they foozled

archibald belonged to a select little golf club, the members of which lived and worked in New York, but played in Jersey. Men of substance, financially as well as physically, they had combined their superfluous cash and with it purchased a strip of land close to the sea. This land had been drained—to the huge discomfort of a colony of mosquitoes which had come to look on the place as their private property—and converted into links, which had become a sort of refuge for incompetent golfers. The members of the Cape Pleasant Club were easy-going refugees from other and more exacting clubs, men who pottered rather than raced round the links; men, in short, who had grown tired of having to stop their game and stand aside in order to allow perspiring experts to whiz past them. The Cape Pleasant golfers did not make themselves slaves to the game. Their language, when they foozled, was gently regretful rather than sulphurous.

P.G. Wodehouse
Archibald's Benefit, Collier's 1910

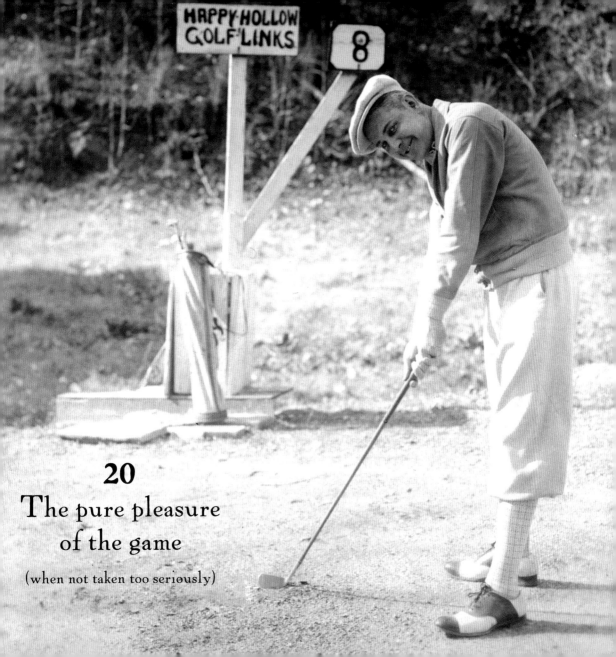

20
The pure pleasure
of the game

(when not taken too seriously)

THE BEAUTY OF NATURE

Strolling on emerald fields amidst magnificent trees, resisting the lure of sparkling lakes and ponds, pausing to admire an ocean vista. In no other sport but golf is the player so directly inspired, challenged, and distracted by nature.

21
The smell of fresh cut grass on a summer morning

22
The hawks soaring around Pinnacle Peak in Scottsdale, Arizona

23
The gulls perched on the railing near the
starter's hut at St. Andrews

24
The birdhouses on Audubon-certified golf courses

25
A giant moose staring at you from
the edge of the woods

26
The intense beauty of a Vermont
course in early October

27

An afternoon spent on a
beautiful golf course brings us
closer to nature.

The 6th green at Coeur d'Alene Golf Course, Idaho

28
Waiting to hit your
approach shot until deer
cross the fairway.

To see one's ball gallop two
hundred and more yards down the
fairway, or see it fly from the face of
an 8-iron clear across an entire copse
of maples in full autumnal flare, is to
join one's soul with the vastness that,
contemplated from another angle,
intimidates the spirit, and
makes one feel small.

John Updike
The Bliss of Golf, from *Golf Dreams*

29

The warmth of the sun, the dry air, and the silence of a remote desert course

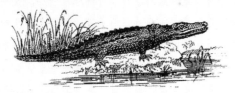

30 An alligator basking in the sun on a Florida course

31 The surf crashing on the rocks around Pebble Beach's 7th green

32 A family of red foxes trotting across the fairway

33 The deep blue Pacific off California's coastal courses

34 A snow-capped mountain range on the horizon

35 The dazzling azaleas at Augusta National Golf Club

36 The moss-draped oaks along an old South Carolina course

37 The dramatic black volcanic rocks on the courses of Hawaii's Big Island

38 Fragrant yellow flowers on the intimidating gorse

39 The coastal marshes of Myrtle Beach

40 The majestic dunes of Ireland's links

41 A fairway running through a forest of tall pines in Northern Michigan

42 The fish that swim with lost golf balls in the lakes and ponds

43 The palm tree-lined fairways of Palm Springs, California

44 Wildflowers behind the green

An Eighteen-Hole Symphony

In playing a round of golf, one experiences an interesting series of physical, emotional, and intellectual waves which are full of significance for the golf architect—waves of exaltation and depression, of excitement and dismay, of wonder and interest, of admiration and irritation, with occasional periods of dead calm, of peacefulness shading perhaps into boredom and monotony. . . The golf architect ought to control these influences with the art and understanding of a musician composing a symphony. Let him become the Beethoven of the golf course, the Mozart of the links, and construct an eighteen-hole symphony!

Theodore Moone
Golf from a New Angle

45
The art and science
of golf architecture

David McLay Kidd's magnificent Bandon Dunes Course, Bandon, Oregon

THE ELEMENTS OF ARCHITECTURE

Nature itself provides the building blocks of a golf course:
green meadows, sandy dunes, trees and brooks, mounds and hollows.
But it's the skill and imagination of the architect
that create a memorable challenge.

60
The strategic challenge of a driving area
squeezed between water and sand

Whirlwind Golf Club at Wild Horse Pass, Phoenix, Arizona

It is an important thing in golf to make holes look much
more difficult than they really are. People get more
pleasure in doing a hole which looks almost impossible,
and yet is not so difficult as it appears.

Alister MacKenzie
Golf Architecture

An early photograph of Cypress Point

61
Alister MacKenzie

Designer of Cypress Point Club, Pasatiempo Golf Club,
Augusta National Golf Club, and Crystal Downs Country Club

62
C.B. MacDonald

Designer of National Golf Links of America,
Long Island, New York

63
Pete Dye

Designer of The TPC at Sawgrass
and The Ocean Course at Kiawah Island

64
Donald Ross

Designer of Pinehurst No. 2 and
Seminole Golf Club

65
A.W. Tillinghast

Designer of Winged Foot Golf Club,
Bethpage State Park (Black Course), and
Baltusrol Golf Club

66
Tom Morris

Designer of Muirfield, Prestwick, St. Andrews
New Course, and Royal Dornoch

67
Jay Morrish

Designer of The Boulders
North and South courses

The Boulders Golf Club, Carefree, Arizona

73
Jack Nicklaus

Designer of Muirfield Village Golf Club, Ohio;
Desert Highlands, Arizona; and Castle Pines, Colorado

74
Jack Neville

Designer of Pebble Beach Golf Links

75
H.S. Colt and George Crump

Designers of Pine Valley

76
Dick Wilson

Designer of Doral's Blue Course and Pine Tree Golf Club

77
William Flynn

Designer of Shinnecock Hills,
Philadelphia Country Club, and Cherry Hills

78
Willie Fernie

Designer of Turnberry Hotel's Ailsa and
Arran courses and Royal Troon

79
Robert Trent Jones, Jr.

Designer of The Prince Course,
Princeville Resort, Kauai, Hawaii

The 16th green on the
challenging Prince Course
at the Princeville Resort

In the rest of our lives perfection is out of reach, an impossible dream; but on a par-3 hole with the wind blowing right, perfection is only an iron away.

Kevin Nelson
The Greatest Golf Shot Ever

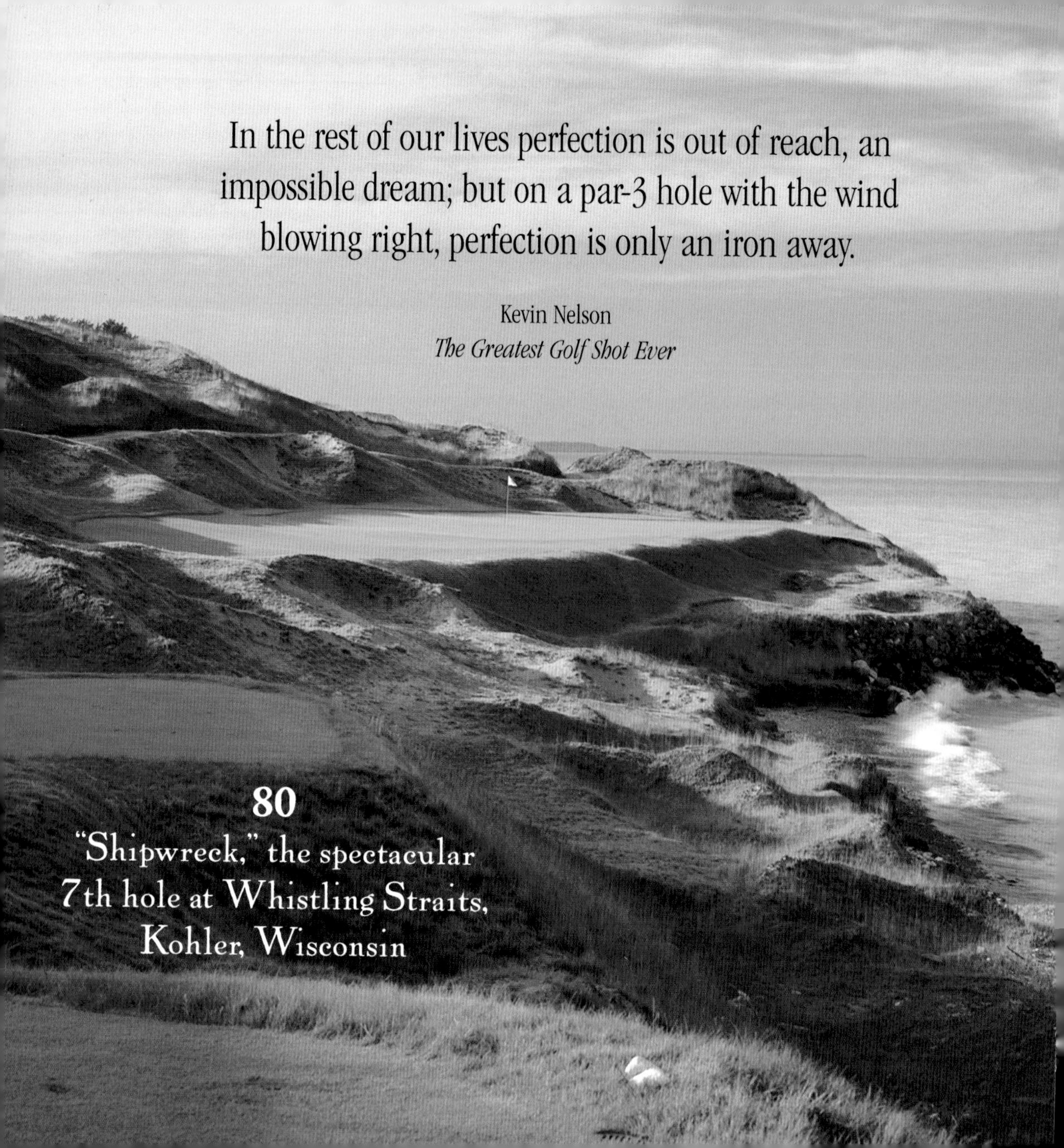

80
"Shipwreck," the spectacular
7th hole at Whistling Straits,
Kohler, Wisconsin

PERFECT PAR-3s

*The possibility of conquering them with a single stroke makes these
beautiful par-3s seductive but dangerous targets.*

81
The 10th hole at Pine Valley, New Jersey

82
The Devil's Cauldron, the 4th hole at Banff Springs

83
The 17th at the TPC at Sawgrass, Stadium Course

84
The Postage Stamp, the 8th hole at Royal Troon, Scotland

85
Golden Bell, the 12th at Augusta National

86
The 233-yard 16th at Cypress Point, California

87
The 3rd hole at Mauna Kea Golf Club, Hawaii

94
The 7th hole at Pebble Beach

A vintage view of the famous 7th hole at Pebble Beach Golf Links

When I get out on that green carpet called
a fairway and manage to poke the ball right
down the middle, my surroundings look
like heaven on earth.

Jimmy Demaret

95
The 6th hole at
Pacific Dunes, Bandon, Oregon

INFAMOUS & BELOVED
BUNKERS

Painful memories notwithstanding, we love these steadfast
opponents. In fact, we like them so much that we give them names.

96
Abandoned Well bunker on the 7th hole at
Tom Doaks's High Pointe Golf Club

97
The Cardinal bunker, 3rd at Prestwick

98
The deadly **Coffins** Bunker, 13th, Hole O'Cross,
St. Andrews Old Course

99
The Devil's Asshole bunker on Pine Valley's 7th

100
Eleanor's Teeth at Apawamis' 4th

110 Hell Bunker, 14th at St. Andrew's Old Course

There is no such thing
as a misplaced bunker.
Regardless of where a bunker
may be, it is the business of the
player to avoid it.

Donald Ross

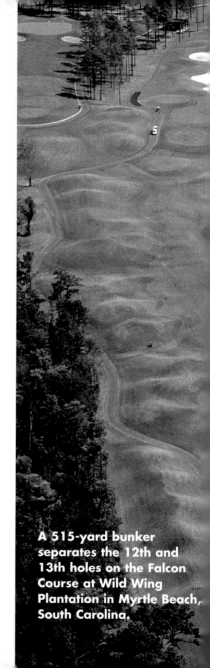

A 515-yard bunker
separates the 12th and
13th holes on the Falcon
Course at Wild Wing
Plantation in Myrtle Beach,
South Carolina.

111
Gaining confidence
with the sand wedge

ISLAND GREENS

Finality is the essence of island greens.
You're either on or it's double bogey—or worse!

119
The floating 14th green at
Coeur D'Alene Resort, Idaho

120

The island fairway on the 5th hole
of Desmond Muirhead's Oak Village Golf Club
near Tokyo, Japan

Oak Village Golf Club's 5th hole

Golf in a Wind

It is a great advantage to have learnt your golf (or to go and learn it) by the sea. Students of the game's history will not need to be informed that nearly all the leading players secured their early training in the pastime on seaside links, or, at any rate, at high and exposed places which the four winds of heaven had claimed among their own playgrounds. The best school of experience is a school in which that gentleman who is known as old Boreas tries to assert authority. Naturally, we do not want half a gale to prevail every time we go out for a round (indeed, humanity is so frail that, if it had any say in the matter, it might vote for the complete suppression of atmospheric disturbance in the region of golf courses), but the fact remains that repeated subjection to a stiff wind helps more than any other influence to make a person a finished golfer. Cricketers and footballers may rise quickly to fame from beginnings made in almost any circumstances—in suburban parks, on patches of waste ground in busy industrial districts, anywhere. An aptitude for golf can

Enjoying the challenge of playing in adverse conditions

hardly fail to make itself manifest at some time or other, and blessed is he who possesses it; but twice blessed is he who has the opportunity to develop it early in life on seaside links. For then necessity will make him the father of invention. There is generally some degree of commotion in the air by the sea, and it has to be circumvented. Not always is it that a plain, straightforward shot achieves the purpose. Ingenuity is stimulated; spin has sometimes to be imparted to the ball so that the wind may be mastered. Then it is that the player learns the higher science of golf; learns how to compel the ball to do anything. When he takes up his abode inland, he may have to practise several new shots (the turf for one thing is generally quite different from that to which he has been accustomed), but with his seaside training he can overcome any difficulty. When a strong wind arises, as it does at times in even the most sheltered places, he is unruffled by it, while the lifelong habitué of the course is perhaps buffeted about in every direction. When, even in the absence of wind, the need presents itself of doing something unusual so as to make the ball curl round an obstacle and reach the chosen spot, the player from the nursery by the sea is usually equal to the occasion.

Harry Vardon
How to Play Golf, 1912

SPECTACULAR
OCEAN HOLES

Nowhere is golf more dramatic than where the land meets the sea. The beauty of the scenery may seduce the golfer into foolish acts of bravery.

131
The famous trio of ocean holes,
the 7th, 8th and 9th at Pebble Beach

132
Ballybunion (old) par-4
11th hole perched on the seaside cliffs

133
Charleston, South Carolina's, Wild Dunes
18th hole, an oceanfront dogleg
along the Atlantic

134
Casa de Campo's "Teeth of the Dog" course
with eight holes on the Caribbean Sea, including
the challenging 5th hole, a par-3 with
a peninsula green

The 3rd hole at Monarch Beach Golf Links, Dana Point, California

Greens near the ocean break imperceptibly toward the sea.

Ben Hogan

135
Scotland's Kingsbarns Golf Links par-5
12th hole that embraces the North Sea

136
Bruce's Castle, the 9th hole on Turnberry's Ailsa course
with the dramatic tee set high on a rocky promontory
at the edge of the sea

137
The 5th hole on the Bay Course at Kapalua
overlooking the Pacific Ocean

138
The magnificent 15th, 16th, and 17th at
Cypress Point bordering the Pacific Ocean

139
Cabo del Sol's spectacular 16th, 17th, and 18th holes
that stretch along the Sea of Cortez

MEMORABLE
FINISHING HOLES

*Finishing holes are where friendly games and big tournaments
are won and lost. That last uphill shot and carry over water towards the
clubhouse are where memories of great rounds are forged.*

159 The 18th at Pebble Beach

160 The view from the clubhouse

On a fine day in the spring, summer, or early autumn, there are few spots more delightful than the terrace in front of our Golf Club. It is a vantage-point peculiarly fitted to the man of philosophic mind: for from it may be seen that varied, never-ending pageant, which men call Golf, in a number of its aspects. To your right, on the first tee, stand the cheery optimists who are about to make their opening drive, happily conscious that even a topped shot will trickle a measurable distance down the steep hill. Away in the valley, directly in front of you, is the lake hole, where these same optimists will be converted to pessimism by the wet splash of a new ball. At your side is the ninth green, with its sinuous undulations which have so often wrecked the returning traveller in sight of home. And at various points within your line of vision are the third tee, the sixth tee, and the sinister bunkers about the eighth green—none of them lacking in food for the reflective mind.

P.G. Wodehouse
The Clicking of Cuthbert

PINEHURST
COUNTRY CLUB

THE ROYAL & ANCIENT

GRAND CLUBHOUSES

*Nowhere is the tradition of the game more apparent than
in its most venerable clubhouses.*

161

The exotic style of the
Medinah Country Club
clubhouse

162

The veranda at The Greenbrier

BALTUSROL

163

The white-columned clubhouse at Pinehurst,
its hallway lined with photos and memorabilia of
outstanding golfers and their feats

164

The mystique of the imposing Royal & Ancient clubhouse
in St. Andrews, with its Royal & Ancient room
filled with a glittering array of trophies
and memorabilia

165

Majestic Baltusrol

166
Congressional Country Club,
Bethesda, Maryland

167 The trophy case in the clubhouse entrance

168 The wood panel engraved with the names of past club champions

169 Locker rooms, where fellowship lives

170 Scorecards of record rounds framed on walls

171 The clubhouse bar, its bottles waiting in neat rows to be summoned to the aid of a fallen ego

172 The golf shop, where we go to buy balls, clubs, gloves, and shoes, and to find a game

173 Hallways lined with old golf prints and early photographs

174

The oldest clubhouse in the United States,
Stanford White's classic design at
Shinnecock Hills Golf Club,
Southampton, New York

WHAT'S IN A NAME?

*Course names draw on history and heritage, a sense of place, local lore,
symbolism, emotions (mostly fear), nature, and of course, humor.*

219

Memories of your hometown golf course

Something about the sight of a fairway

*M*y father took me to Orchard Hills when he deemed me old enough to start learning the game. He woke me up well before dawn on a summer day. He was determined that we should not hold up serious golfers and that we must, therefore, be on the course well before any of them were out of bed. We parked in an empty lot. He stuffed ten dollars for two greens fees into the pro shop mailbox and left a note explaining that we would sign in when we finished the front side.

I don't remember any of the shots I struck that day, though I do recall that my score for nine holes was 78. But I can remember the vista off the first tee. It was a par four with a broad fairway rising to a plateau green. The second hole was a par three heading down from that promontory, with a commanding view of a pond and the green beyond. In my mind's eye the grass at Orchard Hills is velvety and thick, though experience tells me that a municipal course in New Jersey probably had weedy turf chopped up with divot holes.

Velvety or not, I fell instantly in love with that landscape. I liked walking on it. I liked just looking at it. And I have felt the same way about almost every golf course I have seen since then. Something about the sight of a fairway both soothes and excites me.

Bob Cullen
Why Golf?

220
The thrill of playing your
very first round of golf

When I was three, my father put my hands in his and placed them around the shaft of a cut-down women's golf club. He showed me the classic overlap, or Vardon grip—the proper grip for a good golf swing he said—and told me to hit the golf ball...

Hit it hard boy.
Go find it and hit it again.

Arnold Palmer
A Golfer's Life

221 Teaching your children to play

I learned from him how to lose, which is probably more important than how to win.

Arnold Palmer,
*on his father, Deacon Palmer,
the greenskeeper at
Latrobe Country Club*

222
A family golf vacation

223
Father and son tournaments

224
Watching your father hit a long, beautiful drive

225
Buying your grandson his first set of clubs
and taking him to the driving range

226
Cutting down an old 7-iron for your son

227

Playing golf with your dad,
just the two of you

Checked Slacks and Small Courtesies

any men are more faithful to their golf partners than to their wives, and have stuck with them longer. The loyalty we feel toward our chronic consorts in golf acquires naturally the mystical and eternal overtones that the wedding ceremony hopefully, and often vainly, invokes. What is the secret? Structure, I would answer: the golf foursome is constructed with clear and limited purposes denied the nebulously grand and insatiable goals of the marriage twosome.

Like the golf course itself, golf camaraderie is an artifice, carved from the vastness of nature; it asks only five or six hours a week, from the jocular greetings in the noontime parking lot and the parallel donning of cleats in the locker room to the shouted farewells in the dusk, as the flagsticks cast their long shadows. Within this finity, irritations, jealousies, and even spats do occur, but they are mercifully dulled and dampened by the necessary distances of the game, the traditional reticence and mannerliness of sportsmen, and the thought that it will all be soon over. As in marriage, there is sharing: we search for one another's lost balls, we comment helpfully upon one another's defective swings, we march more or less in the same direction, and we come together, like couples at breakfast and dinner, on the tees and on the greens. But unlike marriage, golf is a war from the start: it is out of its regulated contention, its mathematical bloodshed, that the fervor of golf camaraderie blossoms and, from week to week, flourishes. We slay or are slain, eat or are eaten: golf camaraderie is founded on the solid and ancient ground of animal enmity, pleasantly disguised in checked slacks and small courtesies.

John Updike
Golf Dreams,
The Camaraderie of Golf–II

229
A chance to spend time
with good friends

230
Being the first group out on
a crisp spring morning

231
Smacking your tee shot straight down
the fairway after a golfless winter

232
Hitting the sweet spot

233
Fading a high three-iron to
an elevated green

234
Finding your ball in the hole after
looking all around the green

235
Making the first birdie
in a golfing career

236
Each tee shot is a
new beginning

The great Harry Vardon

PIONEERS OF GOLF

These early golfing greats seem to cast a benevolent look on us from above, keeping us from transgressing the rules, or falling into excessive despair or pretense.

Old Tom Morris

237 Old Tom Morris

238 Young Tom Morris

239 Alan Robertson

240 Willie and Mungo Park

241 Willie Anderson

242 John Ball

243 Ted Ray

244 Harry Vardon, J.H. Taylor, and James Braid: The Great Triumverate

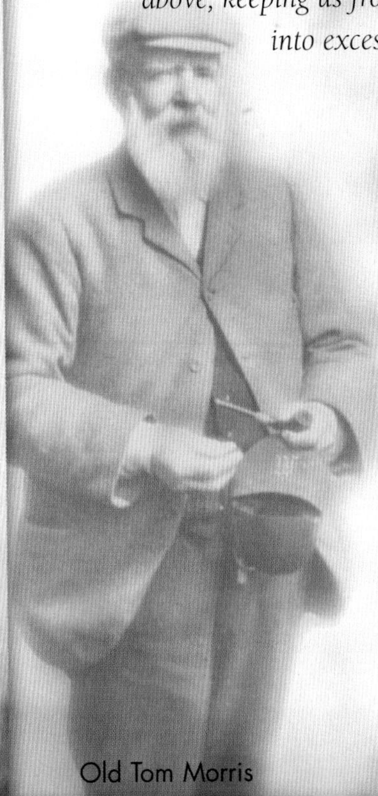

LEGENDS
OF THE GAME

Their stellar championship records and timeless appeal
set these legendary figures apart.

245
Bobby Jones

The game's most inspirational personality. Competing as an amateur,
he won 11 major tournaments including the famous 1930 "Grand Slam."

246
Jack Nicklaus

The greatest golfer ever. Holder of 18 major titles: six Masters, four U.S.
Opens, five PGA Championships, six Ryder Cup titles, and three British Opens.
He also played on six Ryder Cup teams, and was captain for two of them.

247
Arnold Palmer

Charismatic champion and ambassador of golf to the world.
Winner of four Masters, two British Opens and the US Open.

248
Ben Hogan

Perhaps the all-time greatest striker of the ball. Winner of nine
major tournaments including six after his recovery from a
near-fatal car accident.

Bobby Jones and Jack Nicklaus

Gene Sarazen and his wife

249
Gary Player

Golf's globe trotter and winner of over 160 tournaments worldwide including nine major titles.

250
Sam Snead

Ageless champion and golf's most natural ball-striker with a record 81 PGA Tour victories won over six decades. Snead won the Masters and the PGA Championship three times and the British Open once. He was the oldest player to win on the Tour at 52, and the youngest player to shoot his age at 67.

251
Walter Hagen

Winner of 11 major titles with a mixture of style, confidence, and steely nerves.

252
Johnny Miller

Winner of 24 PGA Tour titles, the U.S. Open, and the British Open.

253
Byron Nelson

A great champion, holder of five major titles and forever remembered for his extraordinary 1945 streak of 11 consecutive victories.

254
Gene Sarazen

Holder of 7 major titles including the career "Grand Slam" between 1932 and 1935.

255
Lee Trevino

Colorful personality and winner of two US Opens, two PGA Championships, and back-to-back British Opens.

256
Greg Norman

Winner of two British Opens, the dashing Australian won the hearts of millions around the world for his gracious acceptance of several uncanny defeats in his quest for other major titles.

257
Ben Crenshaw

*Historian of the game, superb putter, and
two-time Masters winner.*

258
Billy Casper

*Winner of 51 PGA Tour events including two
US Opens and one Masters title.*

259
Tom Watson

*Winner of a stunning five British Open titles as well
as two Masters and one US Open. Watson fought
and won several epic battles against Jack Nicklaus.*

260
Nick Faldo

*One of the most fearsome players of the 80s and 90s,
and winner of three Masters and three British Open.*

261
Tiger Woods

*The young man who has changed the face of the
game faster and more profoundly than any other
golfer in history. On his way to becoming the
greatest player ever, unless he is already there.*

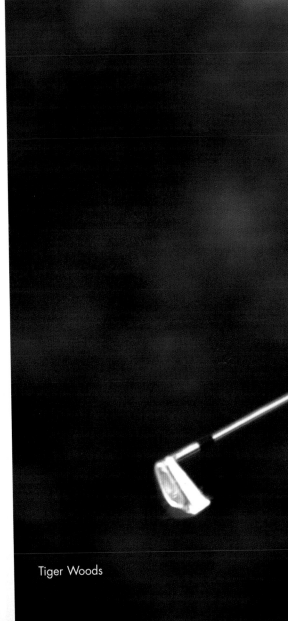

Tiger Woods

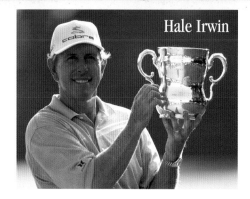

Hale Irwin

CHAMPIONS

They have thrilled us for more than a century of championship golf. They are the heroes we revere and hopelessly try to imitate.

262
Sunday afternoon at the Masters

263
The U.S. Open played at Pebble Beach

264
The traditions of the British Open

265
The drama of the 17th hole at the Tour Championship

266
Sudden-death play-offs

Payne Stewart
Cary Middlecoff
Julius Boros
Lloyd Mangrum
Bernhard Langer
Colin Montgomerie
Tony Jacklin
Chi Chi Rodriguez
Tom Weiskopf
Tom Kite
Jimmy Demaret
Davis Love III
Tommy Armour
Miller Barber
Gene Littler
Vijay Singh
Hale Irwin
Bobby Locke
Sandy Lyle
Fred Couples

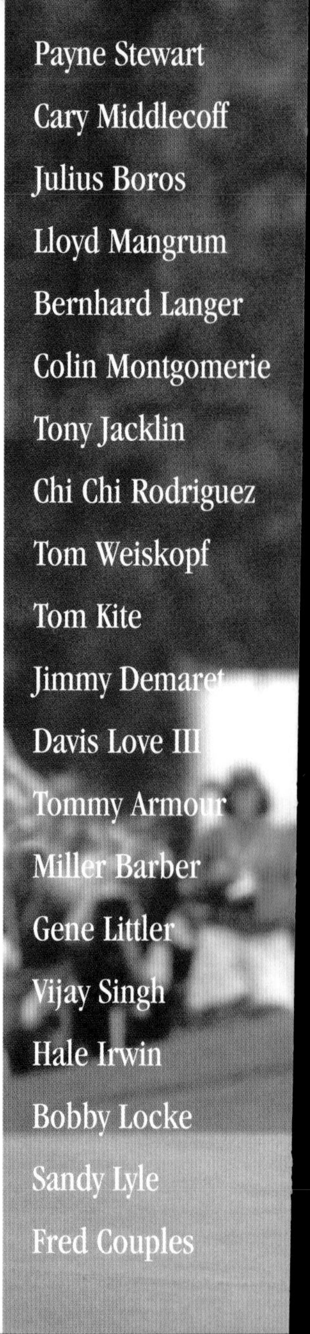

Payne Stewart winning the
1999 U.S. Open at Pinehurst

Phil Mickelson

Craig Stadler

Henry Cotton

Doug Sanders

Fuzzy Zoeller

Jesper Parnevik

John Daly

Sergio Garcia

Ernie Els

Francis Ouimet

Curtis Strange

Hubert Green

Paul Runyan

Lawson Little

Mark O'Meara

Roberto de Vicenzo

Doug Ford

David Graham

Dave Stockton

Ken Venturi

Phil Mickelson

Davis Love III

Sergio Garcia

Corey Pavin

Ian Woosnam

Bob Charles

Lee Janzen

Dow Finsterwald

Tony Lema

Calvin Peete

Lee Elder

Justin Leonard

Retief Goosen

Jose Maria Olazabal

Jim Furyk

Mark Calcavecchia

Tom Lehman

David Duval

Paul Azinger

Nick Price

Royal Dublin Golf Links, circa 1898

267

Golf gives us a chance
to compete with others
while competing
with ourselves.

276
Watching your opponent
three-putt from 10 feet

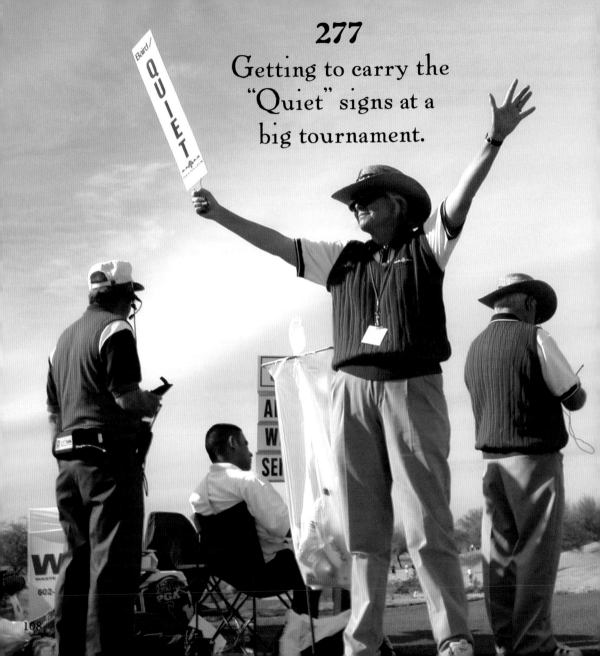

277

Getting to carry the "Quiet" signs at a big tournament.

THE WORLD OF
TOURNAMENT
GOLF

As Bobby Jones once said, "There are two distinct kinds of golf—golf, and tournament golf."

JESPER PARNEVIK

289
Watching a famous pro
at the practice tee

TV—or my TV, anyway—does no justice to the greenness o
Augusta National: an almost hallucinogenic iridescence.
This is what golf in Oz must be like.

Charles McGrath
The Wizard of Oz

290 Golf's biggest challenge, the U.S. Open

291 America's Worst Avid Golfer Tournament

292 Echoes of history at the British Open

293 The AT&T Pebble Beach National Pro-Am
(formerly known as "The Crosby")

294 Sunday afternoon at the Masters, where glory awaits

295 The boat whistles saluting the winner of the Heritage Classic at Hilton Head

296 The Bob Hope Chrysler Classic

297 The Bobby Jones Open
(A charity tournament held in Michigan f anyone named Bob, Robert, or Roberta Jc

298 The Players Championship

299 The rainbow over the PGA Championship when Davis Love III won it in 1997

300 The Colonial

301 The Curtis Cup
(started by American golfing sisters Mar and Harriot Curtis in 1932)

302 The huge crowds enjoying t sunshine at the Phoenix Op

303 The Impregnable Quadrilat
(also known as The Grand Slam)

304
Getting Phil Mickelson to
autograph your shirt

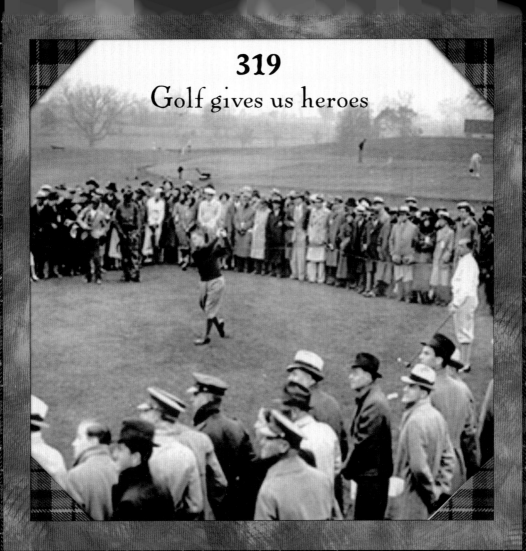

319
Golf gives us heroes

320
Getting ready for the
shotgun start

321
Goodie bags of gifts at
member-guests and
corporate outings

322
Playing with antique clubs at
a hickory stick tournament

323
Surviving the first round of
the club championship

324
Making a crucial putt for
your foursome

325
Winning "closest to the pin"

326
Waiting to hear your name at
an awards ceremony

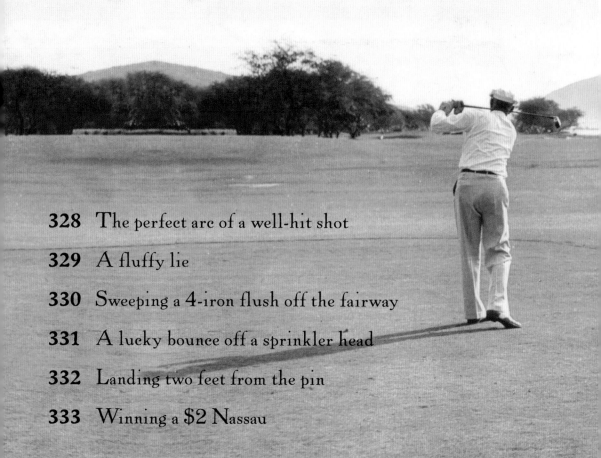

327 Hitting a great drive at the company golf outing

328 The perfect arc of a well-hit shot

329 A fluffy lie

330 Sweeping a 4-iron flush off the fairway

331 A lucky bounce off a sprinkler head

332 Landing two feet from the pin

333 Winning a $2 Nassau

334

A three-day non-stop golf weekend in Myrtle Beach

Wild Wing Plantation's Hummingbird Course,
Myrtle Beach, South Carolina

FARAWAY FAIRWAYS

Show us a brochure of a beautiful golf course in Hawaii, the Rocky Mountains, or the Arizona desert, and we are ready to pack our bags.

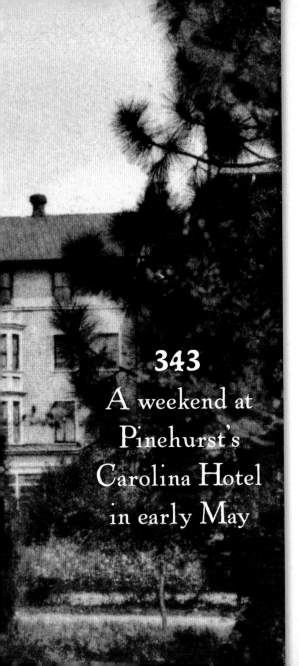

343
A weekend at
Pinehurst's
Carolina Hotel
in early May

Pine Crest Inn Pinehurst, North Carolina

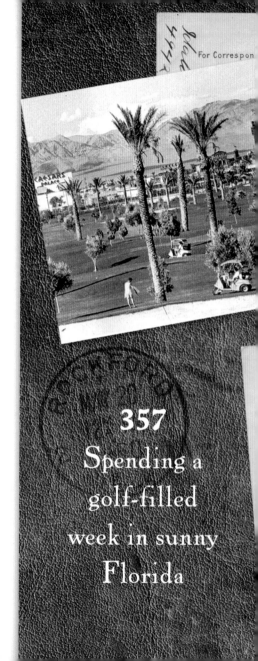

For Correspon

357
Spending a golf-filled week in sunny Florida

358 A bachelor party golf weekend in Las Vegas

Breakers Hotel from Golf Course, Palm Beach, Fla.

359 A golf trip to Gleneagles in Scotland

My car absolutely will not run unless my golf clubs are in the trunk.

Bruce Berlet

360 A golf road trip

361 Dinner at the Holly Inn in Pinehurst, South Carolina

362 A week in February playing golf on the Big Island of Hawaii

363 A corporate convention that just happens to be in Palm Springs

364

Taking a golf cruise

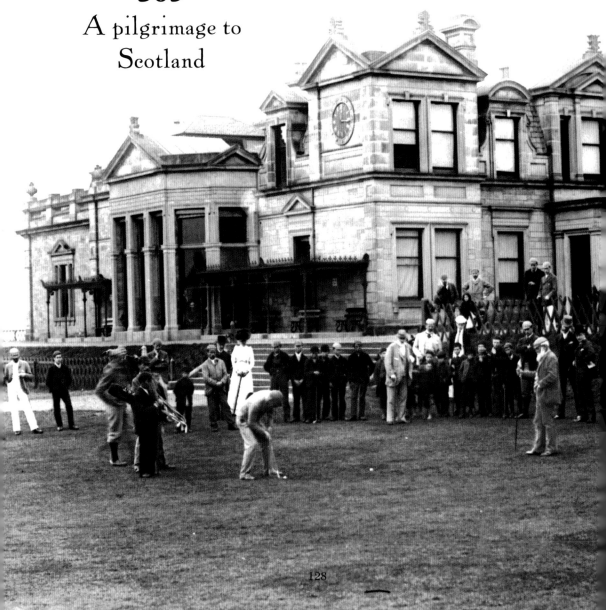

365
A pilgrimage to
Scotland

It is a special feeling, I think, that calls the golfer back to Scotland as the sailor is called by the sea. Take me to the grave of Old Tom Morris, a voice says. Drive me around the Road Hole. Show me where the Wee Icemon chipped it in at Carnoustie. Lead me down the long, narrow 11th at Troon where Arnie made the threes. Let me hear the groan of the spitfire ghosts at Turnberry. Carry me over the Sleepers at Prestwick. Bend me around the archery field at Muirfield. Drown me in all of these treasures of time once more in this, still another life.

Dan Jenkins
The Game of Golfe, from
The Dogged Victims of Inexorable Fate

366
Whales breaching in the dark blue waters
off Kapalua in Hawaii

367
The smell of pine trees on a hot afternoon

368
The otters playing in the waters off Pebble Beach

369
A manatee diving lazily under a
bridge on a Florida course

370
Snowy egrets in a dark cove on a Georgia course

371
Cormorants standing beside ponds, spreading
their wings to dry them in the sun

372
Crows calling from beyond the trees

373
A woodchuck lumbering
across the fairway

130

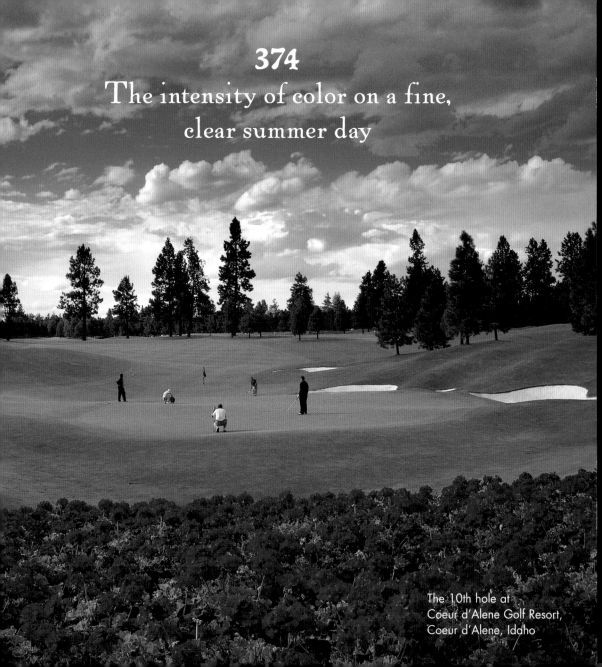

374
The intensity of color on a fine,
clear summer day

The 10th hole at
Coeur d'Alene Golf Resort,
Coeur d'Alene, Idaho

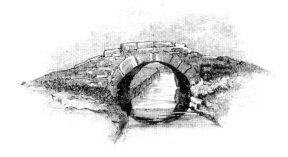

375
Playing St. Andrews' Old Course
for the first time

376
Having a reserved tee time
on the one sunny day of the entire week

377
Being paired with a congenial group of strangers

378
Walking in the footsteps of golf's greats
while crossing the Swilcan Bridge

379
A whisky at the bar on the top floor of
the Old Course Hotel with a view of the
Royal & Ancient clubhouse illuminated
by the setting sun

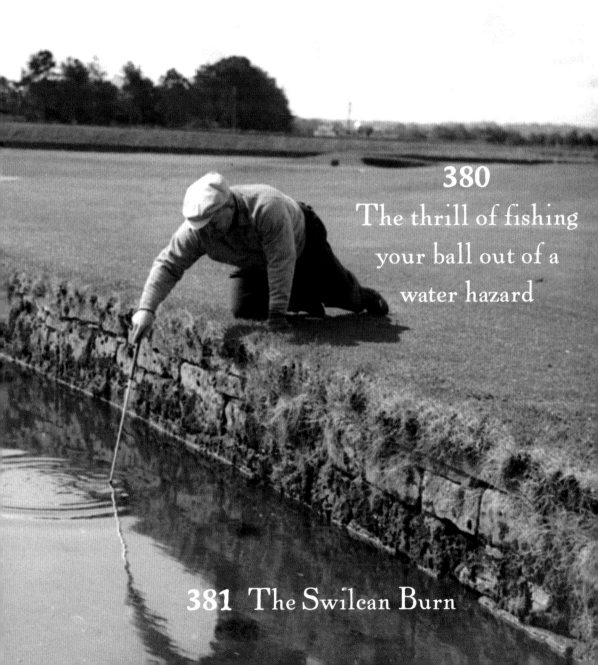

380
The thrill of fishing
your ball out of a
water hazard

381 The Swilcan Burn

382 Getting special attention from the pro

383
Going off to a three day golf school

384
Plaid short shorts

THE PROMISE OF IMPROVEMENT

Learning to play golf is a lifetime affair. Schools, teachers and instruction materials are abundant. Learning a new method or technique is always fun. It might even improve your game…for a while anyway.

385 A new tip that really improves your game

386 Discovering the secret of golf, if only for a few holes

387 A new golf instruction book that promises to shave ten strokes off your short game

388 The enduring wisdom of Bobby Jones's old movies

389 Getting the new issue of *Golf Magazine* in the mail on Saturday morning

390 Researching and selecting the best golf school for you

391 Finding a great golf teacher at the local driving range and taking a lesson on Sunday morning

392 Buying a new set of instruction tapes at the local golf shop

393 Keeping a small notebook of tips and reminders in your golf bag

394 Signing up for a weekend golf school with your best golf buddy

395 Taking your son to Nike Golf Camp for a week

Your final goal is to convert your athletic swing to pure instinct rather than conscious thought.

David Leadbetter

396
Former NASA scientist,
now a renowned golf instructor
and best selling author,
Dave Pelz

OUR FAVORITE
SWING DOCTORS

These eminent golf physicians have a variety of cures for the shanks, the yips, and the dreaded banana ball.

397
Butch
Harmon

406
Harry Vardon

Ben Hogan's POWER

GOLF

AFTER FORTY

HOW TO SCORE UNDER **85** WITH EASE

BY

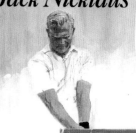

Jack Nicklaus

SWING THE CLUBHEAD

And Cut Your Golf Score

By ERNEST JONES
AND DAVID EISENBERG

HOW THOUSANDS HAVE LEARNED THE SURE WAY TO BETTER

This informal and completely new kind of Instruction Book shows you how to cut strokes from your score by thinking your way around a golf course

A Round of Golf with Tommy Armour

BY THE AUTHOR OF THE CLASSIC BEST SELLER
How to Play Your Best Golf All the Time

SAM SNEAD

HOW TO PLAY GOLF

FOREWORD BY TOM KITE

GOLF IS NOT A GAME OF PERFECT

tion fers PHS to

SECTION—HOW TO
S IN YOUR GOLF SWING

DR. BOB ROTELL
WITH BOB CULLEN

DAVE PELZ
SCORING GAME SERIES

Dave Pelz's Short Game Bible

Foreword by
LEE JANZEN

Master the Finesse Swing
and Lower
Your Score

DAVE PELZ
with
James A. Frank

Bunker Play
Gary Player
WITH MIKE WADE

THE GOLF MASTERS SERIES

THE Golf SECRET

H.A. MURRAY

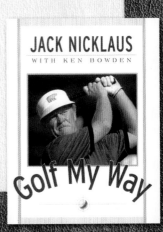

418 Finding your swing

The Secret of Golf

…I stepped up to the ball in a deliberately casual and relaxed fashion and very quietly 'played short.' The ball flew off as though fired from a rifle. I can see it now. It described precisely the trajectory I should have hoped to see with the brassie from a proper lie and finished on the center of the green. I stood rooted to the spot, with feelings akin to those of St. Paul after the episode on the road to Tarsus. Not only had I never played an iron shot like this before: I had never contemplated that the miscellany of muscle, bone, brain and plain avoirdupois that make up my person could ever combine to play such a one—from a fairway, never mind from a divot mark.

I wandered down the fairway as one in a dream. Perhaps at long last this was it. The final revelation. The Secret of Golf.

Henry Longhurst
The Secret of Golf

419
Trying golf hypnosis to
improve your driving

420
Enrolling in a yoga class to get
more flexibility and balance

421
Doing golf meditation to
cure the shanks

422
Resorting to golf affirmations
when all else fails

423
Reading *Be the Ball*, *The
Cosmic Laws of Golf*, *The Inner
Game of Golf*, *Extraordinary Golf*,
and *Golf in the Kingdom* in
search of the answer
to the mystery
of golf

The golfer, like the Hindu mystic, must focus
an enormous amount of concentration in
order to transcend reality.

Eric Nicol and Dave More
Golf: The Agony and the Ecstasy

GOLF
LITERATURE

If you have reached the point where you're ready to give up the game, just reach for a good book. A golf book, of course. At worst, it will prove to you that you are not alone.

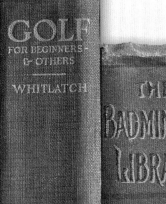

447
Watching the Skins game on TV on a cold winter Sunday

448
Buying gizmos from golf infomercials

449
Tiger Woods's incredible commercials

450
Famous golf TV commentators

451
Criticizing golf TV commentators

452
The Masters on a big screen TV

453
Reruns of *Shell's Wonderful World of Golf*

GOLF IN THE MOVIES

Golf rule number 132: Any movie with golf in it is a great movie

454 Caddyshack *The classic golf comedy starring Chevy Chase, Bill Murray, Ted Knight, and Rodney Dangerfield, 1980*

455 The Legend of Bagger Vance *A disillusioned golfer rediscovers his authentic swing with help from a mystical caddy, Matt Damon and Will Smith, 2000*

456 Tin Cup *A driving range pro tries to qualify for the U.S. Open. Kevin Costner and Rene Russo, 1996*

457 Follow the Sun *Glenn Ford and Anne Baxter in the story of Ben Hogan's near-fatal car accident and miraculous recovery, 1951*

458 Goldfinger *Sean Connery confronts Gert Frobe on the links in a classic golf match, 1964*

459 The Big Broadcast of 1938 *W.C. Fields in a wild golf scene*

460 Pat and Mike *Spencer Tracy and Katherine Hepburn star, with appearances by Babe Zaharias, Betty Hicks, and Helen Dettweiler, 1952*

461 Happy Gilmore *Adam Sandler plays a failed hockey player who joins the PGA Tour, 1996*

462 Dead Solid Perfect *Golf antics on the road, Randy Quaid, 1988*

463 Carefree *Fred Astaire hits golf balls while tap dancing, 1938*

464 Call Me Bwana *Bob Hope is an African explorer who meets Arnold Palmer in the jungle, 1963*

465 Should Married Men Go Home? *Stan Laurel and Oliver Hardy encounter two lovely ladies on the links, 1928*

THAT'S AMORÉ
(That's Love)
Words by JACK BROOKS
Music by HARRY WARREN
SPECIAL PICTURE RELEASE
ONE BIG LOVE
THE GAY CONTINENTAL
IT'S A WHISTLE-IN KINDA MORNIN
THATS AMORÉ
WHAT WOULDCHA DO WITHOUT ME
YOU'RE THE RIGHT ONE
From the Paramount Picture
"THE CADDY"
starring
DEAN MARTIN
and
JERRY LEWIS
with
DONNA REED
PRICE
50¢
in U.S.A.
PARAMOUNT MUSIC CORPORATION • 1619 Broadway • New York 19, N. Y.

OUR FAVORITE
GOLFING CELEBRITIES

There's nothing like watching a celebrity's ball splash into a lake or roll into a deep bunker! Just imagine following these fantasy foursomes.

466
Bing Crosby, Bob Hope, Clint Eastwood & Kevin Costner

467
Howard Hughes, Donald Trump, Bill Gates & Jack Welch

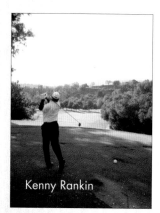

Kenny Rankin

Dinah Shore

468
Andy Williams, Cheech Martin,
Alice Cooper &
Lawrence Welk

469
Kenny Rankin, Willie Nelson,
Vince Gill & Glen Frey

470
Jack Lemmon, Glen Campbell,
Chevy Chase & Oliver Hardy

One minute it's
fear and loathing,
but hit a couple of
good shots and
you're on top of
the world.
I've gone crazy
over this game.

Jack Nicholson

Bob Hope's swing? I've seen better swings
on a condemned playground.
Bing Crosby

Bing was a man who took his golf very seriously.

Bob Hope

Bing Crosby tees off at St. Andrews

Catherine Zeta-Jones

471
Bryant Gumble,
Maury Povich,
Bill Clinton
& Rush Limbaugh

472
Groucho Marx,
Leslie Nielsen,
Jackie Gleason
& Bill Murray

473
Jane Seymour,
Celine Dion,
Dinah Shore
& Susan Anton

474
Michael Jordan,
Mickey Rooney,
Deepak Chopra
& Yogi Berra

475

Dean Martin,
Frank Sinatra,
Sammy Davis Jr.
& Joey Bishop

476

George Burns,
Jack Benny,
Sean Connery
& Johnny Carson

477

Michael Douglas,
Catherine Zeta-Jones,
Jack Nicholson
& Kirk Douglas

Michael Douglas

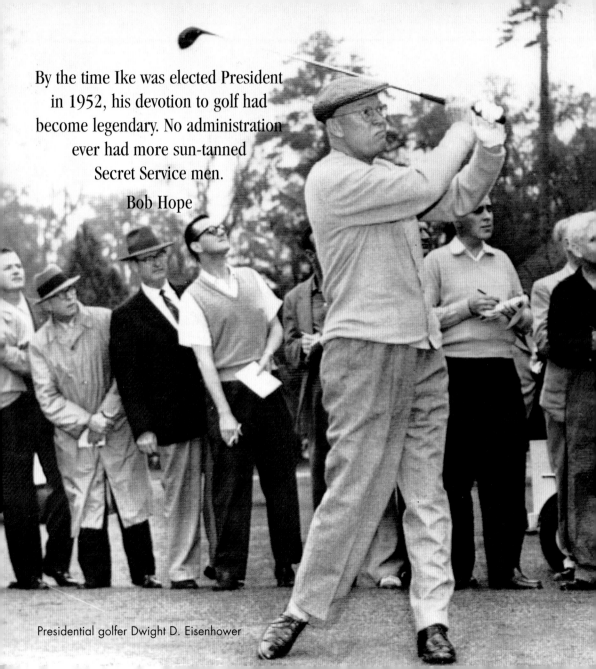

By the time Ike was elected President in 1952, his devotion to golf had become legendary. No administration ever had more sun-tanned Secret Service men.

Bob Hope

Presidential golfer Dwight D. Eisenhower

GOLFING
PRESIDENTS

*Making difficult strategic choices, attempting heroic shots,
and avoiding bunkers are necessary skills for anyone
holding the land's highest political office.*

In the Wake of a Slow Foursome

Every golfer who ever conceded himself a two-foot putt because he was afraid he might miss it has sweated and suffered and blasphemed in the wake of **a slow foursome.** All the clubs that I have ever seen—and I've traveled a bit—are cursed with at least one of these **creeping pestilences** which you observe mostly from the rear.

Nobody knows why they never look behind them. Nobody knows why they never hear any one yell "Fore!"

You're a golfer, of course, and you know the makeup of a slow foursome as well as I do: four nice old gentlemen, prominent in business circles, church members, who remember it even when they top a tee shot, pillars of society, rich enough to be carried over the course in palanquins, but **too proud to ride, too dignified to hurry,** too meek to argue except among themselves, and too infernally selfish to stand aside and let the younger men go through. **They take nine practice swings before hitting a shot, and then flub it disgracefully;** they hold a prayer meeting on every putting green and a postmortem on every tee, and a rheumatic snail could give them a flying start and beat them out in a fifty-yard dash. Know 'em? What golfer doesn't?

But nobody knows why it is that the four slowest players in every club always manage to hook up in a sort of permanent alliance. Nobody knows why they never stage their creeping contests on the off days when the course is clear. Nobody knows why they always pick the sunniest afternoons, when the locker room is full of young men dressing in a hurry. Nobody knows why they bolt their luncheons and scuttle out to the first tee, nor where that speed goes as soon as they drive and start down the course. Nobody knows why they refuse to walk any faster than a **bogged mooley**

492
Playing 18 holes in less than four hours

The fast-walking, quick-swinging fellows lose because the slow foursome blocks the way.

cow. Nobody knows why they never look behind them. Nobody knows why they never hear any one yell "Fore!" Nobody knows why they are so dead set against letting any one through.

Everybody knows **the fatal effect of standing too long over the ball,** all dressed up with nowhere to go. Everybody knows of the tee shots that are slopped and sliced and hooked; of the indecision caused by the long wait before playing the second; of the change of clubs when the first choice was the correct one; of the inevitable penalty exacted by loss of temper and mental poise. Everybody knows that a slow foursome gives the Recording Angel a busy afternoon, and leaves a sulphurous haze over an entire course. But the aged reprobates who are responsible for all this

trouble—**do they care how much grief and rage and bitterness simmers in their wake?** You think they do? Think again. Golf and Business are the only games they have ever had time to learn, and one set of rules does for both. The rest of the world may go hang! Golf is a serious matter with these hoary offenders, and they manage to make it serious for everybody behind them—the fast-walking, quick-swinging fellows who are out for a sweat and a good time and lose both because the slow foursome blocks the way.

Charles E. Van Loan
Fore! 1914

493 The peacefulness of a solitary round

494 A magical day when every putt goes in

495
Walking 18 holes carrying
a light shoulder bag

496
The time spent reflecting between shots

If an average golfer takes **90 shots** in a round, and each shot takes about **two seconds**, that adds up to only about **three minutes of actual play.** The pre-shot routine takes anywhere from **five to ten seconds**, which adds another **ten minutes** or so. That leaves more than **three hours and forty-five minutes** of time between shots in a typical four-hour round—about 95 percent of the round. This is time when you are **simply out on the course, walking** (or riding) to your next shot.

Fred Shoemaker
*Extraordinary Golf:
The Art of the Possible*

THE OBSERVANCE OF TRADITIONAL
GOLF ETIQUETTE

While other sports celebrate their lack of refinement,
golf still has certain unwritten, but expected, courtesies.

497 Silence is golden when someone else is playing

498 Keeping up the pace of play

499 Transcending the rules and adopting the concept of "Ready Golf" to keep the game moving along without delay

500 Leaving the green and discussing the scores on the next tee

501 Calling a penalty on yourself

502 Following the rules when playing alone

503 Being ready to hit when it's your turn

504 Staying still when another player is putting

505 Not standing in a player's backswing line of sight

506 Being considerate of the golf course and the work done by the maintenance crews

507 Never hitting a shot into or close to the group ahead

508 Allowing a faster group to play through

509 Not leaving behind your ciga and cigarette butts, or any tra

510 Raking bunkers, replacing divots and fixing pitchmarks

511 Long, late afternoon shadows that stretch across the fairway

Branson Creek Golf Club, Branson, Missouri

Princeville's Prince Course, 12th hole

512
Breathing in the cool, fresh Atlantic air on a remote Canadian Maritimes course

513
The dew shining on the greens in the early morning

514
A bright, clear, fast-moving brook that races alongside a mountain fairway

515
Bright, warm sunshine after a thunderstorm

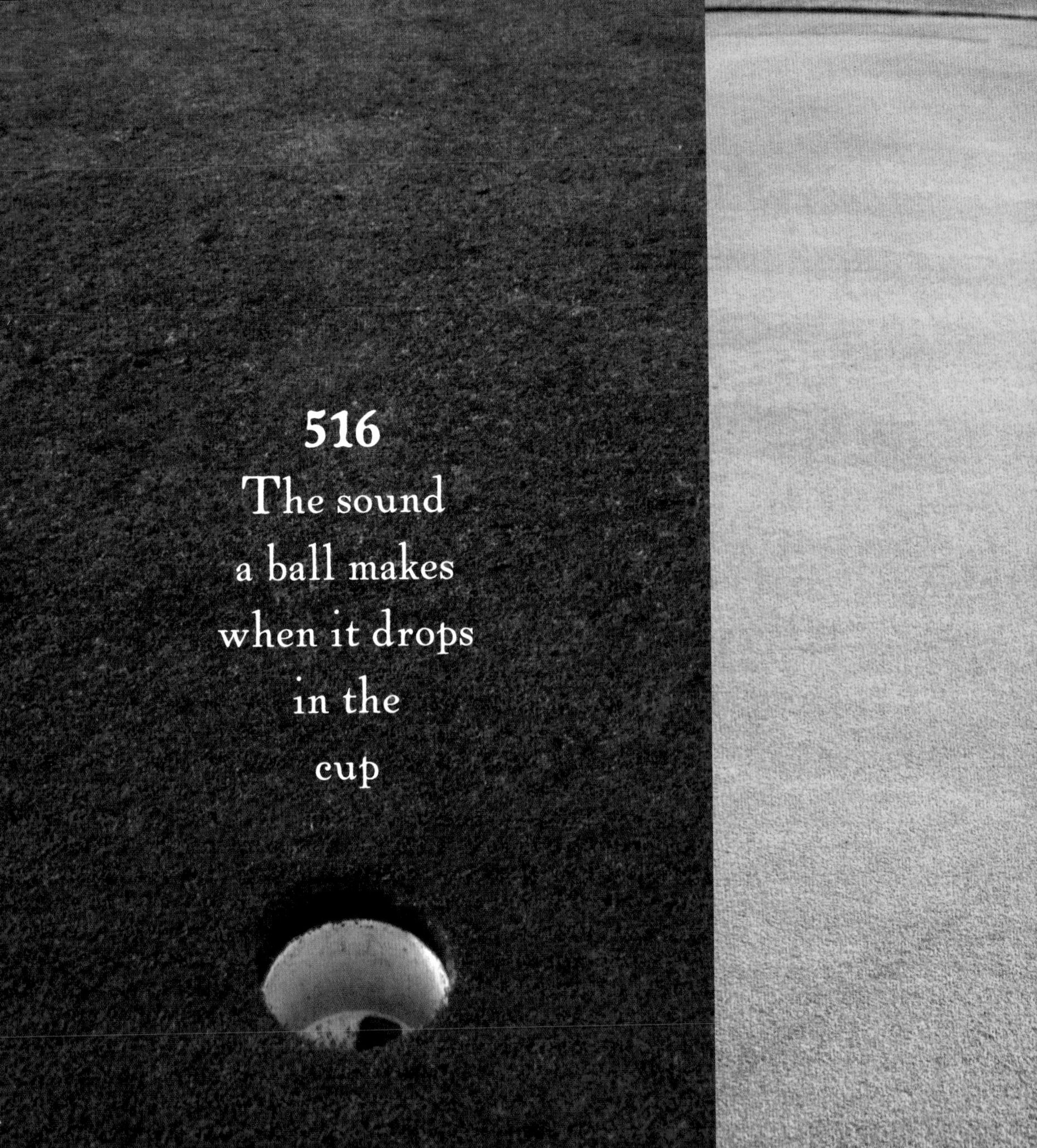

516
The sound
a ball makes
when it drops
in the
cup

517 All shades of green

PRESERVING GOLF'S HISTORY & TRADITIONS

Golf museums, societies and associations range from the traditional and all-business to the literary and whimsical. But, it's all for the love of the game!

533 The United States Golf Association

THE LANGUAGE OF GOLF

To the beginner, golfspeak may sometimes sound more arcane than Latin and Greek. Yet, it does not take long for the words to come naturally.

air-shot: *a shot that misses the ball*

army golf: *left, right, left, right*

banana ball: *ball curving severely to the right*

beach: *sandtrap*

big dog: *driver*

birdie: *one below par*

blades: *irons*

bogey: *one over par*

breakfast ball: *mulligan after breakfast*

center cut: *a putt to the center of the hole*

chili-dip: *hitting the ground instead of the ball*

chunk: *same as the chili-dip*

cozy: *very close to the hole*

cup: *the hole*

dance floor: *putting green*

dew sweepers: *early morning players*

dogleg: *a hole which turns left or right*

dormie: *to be enough ahead in a match so that one cannot lose*

duffer: *a mediocre golfer*

draino: *a long putt*

drink: *water hazard*

emergency room: *the bar*

fat (shot): *hitting the ground before the ball*

foozle: *a bungled shot*

foot wedge: *kicking the ball out of trouble (against the rules)*

fried egg lie: *ball half buried in the sand*

gimme: *a very short putt*

golf lawyer: *golfer who applies all the rules*

534
Golf talk

THE GAME SCOTCHMEN KNOCK "L" OUT OF.

golf widow: *a golfer's spouse*

hook: *a shot that curves to the left*

jungle: *rough*

leaner: *a ball that leans against the flagstick but doesn't drop into the hole*

mulligan: *a penalty-free second drive*

Nassau: *Bet placed on first nine holes, second nine, and full round*

O.B.: *out-of-bounds*

pill: *ball*

pin: *flagstick*

rainmaker: *a very high tee-shot*

sandbagger: *golfer with artificially high handicap*

sandy: *making par from a bunker*

skull: *to hit the top of the ball*

skyball: *excessively high shot*

slice: *a shot that curves to the right*

smiler: *ball with a cut*

snowman: *score of 8*

spoon: *early name for a three-wood*

stick: *golf club*

stymie: *a putt with your opponent's ball lying between your ball and the hole*

swing doctor: *golf teacher*

swing oil: *beer*

Texas wedge: *putting from off the green*

tweeter: *birdie*

water ball: *worn out ball used to play over water*

whiff: *to miss the ball entirely*

wind-cheater: *low-trajectory shot*

worm-burner: *ground ball*

yips: *nervous affliction that causes a golfer to freeze over an important putt*

you da man!: *golf expression favored by enthusiastic fans at tournaments*

THE BALL THAT SCIENCE BUILT AGAIN LEADS THE FIELD

With its exclusive Silicone "*Magic*" center... a development of U.S. Rubber scientists using General Electric Silicone.

With its famous *Electronic Winding*...for uniformity, accuracy and controllability.

With its *Cadwell-Geer Cover*... the toughest and most responsive ever made.

The greatest driving, hitting and putting golf ball in the history of the game.

GOLF SCIENCE
& INVENTORS

The trajectory of the golf ball is dictated by the laws of physics, at least generally speaking. Many scientific geniuses and clever inventors have been working out the details for us.

535
Gene Sarazen, inventor of the sand wedge in 1932

536
Karsten Solheim's individual style and scientific genius

537
The World Scientific Congress of Golf Trust

538
African-American dentist, George E. Grant, who patented the tapered golf tee in 1899

539
Coburn Haskell, inventor of the Haskell Ball, the first golf ball with rubber thread wound around a solid core

540
Joe Garske, creator of the Par Aide
ball washer in 1955

541 Dentist William Lowell who designed and patented the "Reddy Tee," in 1924

542 Iron Byron, the mechanical golfer of the USGA

543 Jack Jolley, inventor of the liquid center ball

544 Tom Mascaro, inventor of the Aerifier (1946) and the Verti-Cut (1955), as well as more than 100 turf-related devices

545 Ted Jorgensen's book, *The Physics of Golf*

546 Faris McMullin, inventor of the plastic golf cleat, or soft spike, in 1991

547 Frank Thomas, inventor of the graphite shaft

548 William Taylor, inventor of the dimpled golf ball, 1930s

549 Gary Adams, co-founder of Taylor Made and credited as the "father" of the modern metal wood

550 Dr. Glenn Burton, the developer of Tiflawn bermuda, the first grass variety designed especially for fairways, in 1952

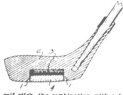

985,194. GOLF-STICK. JOHN MARSHALL McLAREN, Sandringham, near Melbourne, Victoria, Australia, assignor of one-half to Perry R. Chance, Tacoma, Wash. Filed Jan. 27, 1910. Serial No. 540,303.

1. In a golf stick, the combination with a head having a cavity formed in the lower side thereof and extending upward a part way therethrough; unit weights within the cavity and occupying only a portion thereof; and a plug filling the remainder of the cavity and cemented therein and engaging the end of the weight to prevent the movement thereof within the cavity.

2. In a golf stick, the combination with a head having a cylindrical cavity formed in its lower side and extending upward a part way therethrough; dished metal disks therein, of smaller diameter than the cavity, and each forming a unit weight; and a plug adapted to be driven into said cavity and to flatten said disks to spread them into contact with the cavity walls.

The original Par Aide ball washer

The Venturi Effect*

A speeding, spinning ball is subject to the VENTURI EFFECT, meaning that an increase in the velocity of a flow of air decreases its cross-sectional pressure. The air passing over (A) that portion of the ball that is turning with the passing air will move faster than the air passing over (B) that portion of the ball that is turning against the passing air. Therefore the air at "A" will exert less pressure than the air at "B" so the ball will be pushed in the direction of "A." If portion "A" is above the center, the pressure from "B" will produce a vertical lift. If "A" leans to either side of the vertical, the pressure at "B" will produce a sidewise push toward "A." If "A" is toward the player's left it will produce a hook—to his right, a slice. But the action will be definite—not wavering. Predictable and controllable. The more airspeed, the more effect for any given amount of spin. Without backspin, the ball will wobble along erratically. And the dimpled cover greatly magnifies this wobble control. So it follows, that a Ball with "Overspin" has no "Lift"—the "Duck Hook." A truly well hit Ball from any Club will

* A venturi is a short, tapered tube or nozzle and oddly enough has nothing to do with the golfer, Ken Venturi.

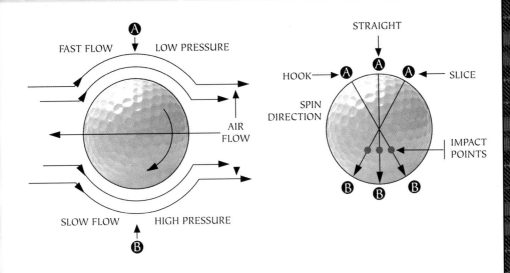

have a higher trajectory than otherwise, simply because the increased velocity and Backspin will lengthen the upward portion of the flight. In addition, when there is Clubface "Layback" during Impact, the additional height will be even more noticeable as the Impact Interval lengthens. And ALWAYS— the more Compression Leakage, the more faulty the Angle of Separation that is, lower trajectory and less distance.

Homer Kelley
The Golfing Machine, 1969

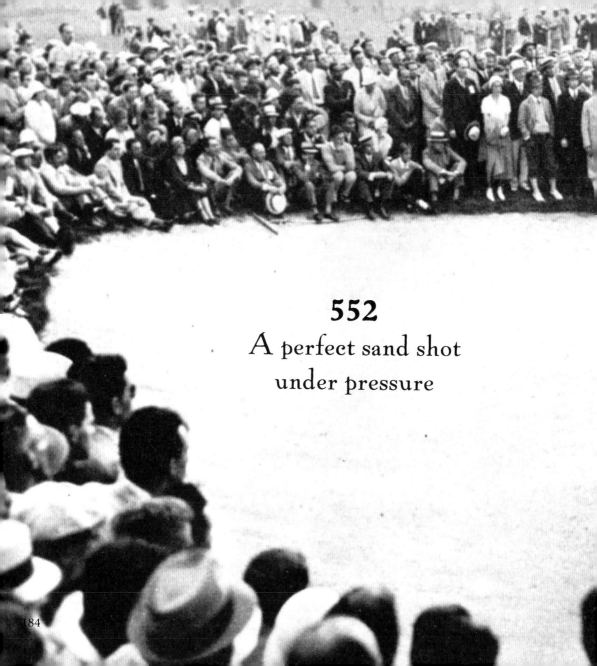

552

A perfect sand shot
under pressure

Gene Sarazen pitching to the green on the final hole of the 1932 British Open

I n the town of New Port Richey, on the west coast of Florida, where (Sarazen) and his wife then spent their winters, there was a mechanic at a local garage who was particularly good at soldering. Sarazen bought up all the solder at the local hardware store, and, at his direction, the mechanic applied it to the soles of twelve niblicks that Sarazen had collected. Sarazen then took the clubs out to a bunker on an abandoned course nearby and, shaping the solder with rasps and files—and sometimes adding more solder back at the garage—kept experimenting until he arrived at what he was after: a club with a heavy, wide flanged sole that, when it struck the sand behind the ball, exploded the ball out of good lies, bad lies, and buried lies with an efficiency far beyond that of the niblick, the club traditionally used in bunkers. The new club was the first sand wedge. It soon became a standard club in every golfer's bag. It was in Sarazen's bag in 1932 when he reclaimed his position at the forefront of golf by winning both the British Open and our Open in the same year—an exploit that only Jones had brought off before him.

Herbert Warren Wind
Following Through

553
Ben Hogan's
New York
ticker tape parade
in 1953

UNFORGETTABLE
MOMENTS

*Only a lucky few were able to witness these achievements
in person. But thanks to photography, television and great
sports writers, millions of us can enjoy the memory of
many defining moments in the history of the game.*

554
Young American amateur Francis Ouimet's
astounding playoff victory over veteran British
professionals Harry Vardon and Ted Ray
in the 1913 U.S. Open

555
Arnold Palmer's 360-yard drive to
the first green of the 1960 US Open
at Cherry Hills

556
Ben Crenshaw's tearful second win
at the 1995 Masters

557
Ben Hogan's one-iron on the 18th
at Merion in the 1950 US Open

Bobby Jones poses for photogrraphers after
1930 British Amateur victory at St. Andrews

558 Bob Tway's hole-out birdie from a bunker on the final hole of the 1986 PGA Championship

559 Bobby Jones' two tickertape parades down Broadway in 1926 and 1930

560 Gene Sarazen's double eagle on the 15th at Augusta during the 1935 Masters

561 Jack Nicklaus' 1972 U.S. Open one-iron on the 17th at Pebble Beach

562 Jack Nicklaus' historic sixth victory at the 1986 Masters

563 Tom Weiskopf's 13 on the par-3 12th at Augusta

564 Larry Mize's stunning chip-in at the 1987 Masters

565 Arnold Palmer's emotional goodbye to St. Andrews in the summer of 2000

566 Tiger Woods' first Masters Tournament win in 1997 at the age of 21. His 12-stroke lead was the widest margin of victory in Masters Tournament history

567 February 6, 1971: Alan Shepard's golf shot on the moon

568 Tom Watson's dramatic victory over Nicklaus at Turnberry in the 1977 British Open

569 Tom Watson's chip-in from the rough at Pebble Beach's 17th in the 1982 U.S. Open

The moment he'd waited for
all his golfing life

One more par, just one more par—that's what he wanted at 18. He had a two-stroke cushion over Nicklaus and over Souchak, who had just parred number 16. Fleck, now playing the 16th, was his closest pursuer, just one stroke behind. Cherry, back on the 15th hole, faced a two-stroke deficit.

Palmer hit a one-iron from the 18th tee across the pond and safely onto the fairway. His second shot, a four-iron, came up short and to the left of the green. He was 80 feet from the pin and in the rough. If he took three to get down, one of his pursuers might still catch him. If he got down in two, he'd have his 280, and somebody would have to get hot to catch him. This was the moment he'd waited for all his golfing life.

Arnold hit the perfect chip shot. It ran up two-and-a-half feet of the pin. Walking to his ball, he casually repaired a ball mark, then surveyed his line. When he bent over his ball to putt, he said later, it seemed like a 25-footer. In the long shadows of the late Denver afternoon, Arnold Palmer rolled it home. He took two quick steps forward, scooped it up out of the cup, and without breaking stride he peeled off his red sun visor and pitched it high in the air toward the gallery at the back of the green. Palmer, beaming, looked like some happy kid half his age. On NBC's videotaped broadcast, an announcer cried, "Palmer has won! Palmer has won!" But it wasn't over.

Julian I. Graubart
Golf's Greatest Championship: The 1960 U.S. Open

190

570
Arnold Palmer's
legendary charge to victory on
the last round of the 1960
U.S. Open at Cherry Hills

571
The miracle
of a hole-in-one

*A*ces are always a surprise, sometimes even after you hit one. You hit it, lose track of the ball, search for it, give up, then discover it . . . in the hole. It is a revelation that does not unfold itself immediately— rather, in stages, like the petals of a flower opening toward the sun.

Kevin Nelson
The Greatest Golf Shot Ever Made

THE COURSES WE
DREAM ABOUT

*They are on the list of courses all dedicated golfers would
like to play once in a lifetime. Distance, expense and
exclusivity keep them out of reach of the ordinary woman
and man, except when we close our eyes and
step up on their imaginary first tee.*

572
Cypress Point Club

596
The Boulders

616
The 8th hole at Prairie Dunes Golf and Country Club,
Hutchinson, Kansas

For many golfers, a round at Pine Valley is the game's Holy Grail. Jack Nicklaus famously played it on his honeymoon, leaving his new bride in the car.

David Owen
My Usual Game

An early photograph of the 2nd hole at Pine Valley

617 The infamous Pine Valley

CLASSIC LINKS

*Amidst the grassy mounds and sandy hollows of the links course,
a golfer must duel against stiff ocean breezes, unpredictable bounces
and occasional dreadful situations. Tenacity and a combination
of power, technique and imagination is required to vanquish
this tenacious foe. But nowhere is the beauty of the game
so raw and so compelling.*

618
The challenge and beauty
of seaside links

A Treeless Sweep of Billowing Pale-green Land

At first glance, even the most distinguished linksland courses look utterly ordinary to the man who has never played them before. If a golfer stands on the terrace at the Augusta National Golf Club, say, and takes in the wide panorama of lush fairways swinging through tall pines, he senses at once that an authentic championship layout awaits him—an experience that also occurs at most of the world's renowned inland courses. But let him stand on the first tee at St. Andrews or Ballybunion, and all he sees is a treeless sweep of billowing pale-green land with a few dun-colored sand hills in the distance—a most unpromising vista. A fragment of fairway is visible here and another fragment there, and a few numbered flags are blowing in the breeze, so what he is looking at is evidently a golf course, but it might as easily be pastureland. It is only when the golfer gets out onto a linksland course that he discovers, to his amazement, that it is filled with great golf holes, all the more appealing since their strategic features were molded by nature instead of by the bulldozer.

Herbert Warren Wind
Following Through

619
The natural quirks of a
true links golf course

UNIQUE
HOLE NAMES

Thinking of walking across the Sahara or climbing the Himalayas? A visit to a nearby golf course might be the easiest way to get there. From The Devil's Cauldron to Elysian Fields, from The Suez Canal to the San Andreas Fault, these golf holes each have a character all their own

620 **The Devil's Cauldron,** the 4th at Banff Springs Golf Course

621 **Alcatraz**, the 17th at PGA West Stadium Course

622 *The Suez Canal,* hole #14 at Royal St. George's in Sandwich, England

623 AMEN CORNER, holes #11 (White Dogwood), 12 (Golden Bell) & 13 (Azalea) at Augusta National

624 **fin' me oot,** Turnberry's 5th

625 Himalayas, the 5th hole at Prestwick

626 THE ALPS, hole #17 at Prestwick

627 **The Postage Stamp**, Royal Troon's 8th hole

628 South America, Carnoustie's 10th h

629 **Ginger Beer**, the 4th hole at St. Andrews Old Course

630 **Hell's Hole**, the 5th hole at Crail Golfing Society Balcomie Links

631 **DEATH OR GLORY**, hole #7 at Hayling in England

632 PUNCHBOWL, the 9th hole at Royal Liverpool

633 calamity, #14 at Royal Portrush

634 **Purgatory,** #15 at Royal Portrush

635 *Tranquility,* #11 at Waterville

636 *Shipwreck,* #16 at Tralee

LEGENDARY WOMEN CHAMPIONS

*We celebrate the outstanding achievements
of the great women of golf.*

✥

662
Babe Didrikson Zaharias

*All-American basketball player, winner of two gold medals
and a silver medal in the 1932 Olympics in track and field,
Babe was a true all-around athlete. Turning to golf in the
1930's, she would go on to win 82 tournaments in her
dazzling 20 year career in golf. A founding member of the
LPGA, she was one of the first four inductees into
the LPGA Hall of Fame in 1951.*

663
Kathy Whitworth

Winner of a record 88 LPGA events

664
Patty Berg

*Pioneer of ladies professional golf and holder of more than
80 amateur and professional victories*

Babe Didrikson Zaharias

Nancy Lopez

665
Louise Suggs
Winner of 50 LPGA events and one of the founders of the LPGA

666
Betty Jameson
1947 National Open champion and first woman to break 300 in a 72-hole tournament

667
Joyce Wethered
Leading player of the '20s and '30s. "The best golfer I have ever seen," according to Bobby Jones

668
Nancy Lopez
Popular golfer Nancy Lopez was named Rookie of the Year in 1977, LPGA Player of the Year four times, and won the LPGA Championship three times. She was inducted into the LPGA Hall of Fame in 1987.

Joyce Wethered

669
Mickey Wright

Four-time winner of both the U.S. Women's Open and the LPGA Championship. Between 1959 and 1968, Wright won 79 tournaments, setting a record of 13 victories in 1963 alone. Voted Woman Athlete of the Year in 1963 and 1964, she was inducted into the LPGA Hall of Fame in 1964 and the World Golf Hall of Fame in 1976.

670
Betsy Rawls

Winner of more than fifty tournaments including four U.S. Women Opens and two LPGA Championships

Mickey Wright

671
Annika Sorenstam

Since joining the LPGA Tour in 1994, Annika Sorenstam has established herself as one of the most steadfast champions women's golf has ever known. Besides accumulating a vast and glittering collection of prestigious trophies and distinctions, Annika is the first woman ever to record a round of 59 in an official LPGA Tour event.

672
JoAnne Carner
Winner of 42 LPGA events, she was inducted into the LPGA Hall of Fame in 1982

Other LPGA Favorites

673
Patty Sheehan

674
Betsy King

675
Sandra Haynie

676
Carol Mann

677
Judy Rankin

678
Juli Inkster

679
Beth Daniel

680
Donna Caponi

681
Amy Alcott

682
Glenna Collett Vare
"The Female Bobby Jones," six-time winner of
the U.S. Amateur and numerous other titles

Glenna Collett Vare at Pebble Beach

683
The Black Scot
(young Tommy Armour)

FAMILIAR GOLF NICKNAMES

Golf's roster of champions abounds with colorful personalities, fascinating characters and unique styles. Nicknames express our fondness for these beloved champions.

684 The Squire *(Gene Sarazen)*

685 The King *(Arnold Palmer)*

686 The Father of Golf
(Tom Morris)

687 The Silver Scott
(Tommy Armour)

688 The Wee Ice Mon
(Ben Hogan)

689 The Hawk *(Ben Hogan)*

690 Slammin' Sammy
(Sam Snead)

691 Thunder Bolt *(Tommy Bolt)*

692 Titanic Thompson
(Alvin Clarence Thomas)

693 The Shark *(Greg Norman)*

694 The Merry Mex
(Lee Trevino)

695 The Walrus *(Craig Stadler)*

696 Boom Boom *(Fred Couples)*

697 Sir Walter *(Walter Hagen)*

698 The Haig *(Walter Hagen)*

699 Doc *(Cary Middlecoff)*

700 The Joplin Ghost
(Horton Smith)

701 Wild Bill Melhorn
(William Melhorn)

702 Big Cat *(Evan Williams)*

703 Lord Byron *(Byron Nelson)*

704 Champagne Tony
(Tony Lema)

705 Terrible Tom *(Tom Weiskopf)*

706 Little Poison *(Paul Runyan)*

707 Mr. 59 *(Al Geiberger)*

708 Long Jim *(James Barnes Sr.)*

709 Rossie *(Bob Rosburg)*

710 Gentle Ben *(Ben Crenshaw)*

711 Jacko *(Tony Jacklin)*

712 Monty *(Colin Montgomerie)*

713 El Niño *(Sergio Garcia)*

714 The Big Easy *(Ernie Els)*

715 The Golden Bear
(Jack Nicklaus)

716 Mr. November *(Mike Weir)*

717 The Black Knight
(Gary Player)

718 Snake *(Greg Chalmers)*

719 Pipeline Moe *(Moe Norman)*

720 Double-D *(David Duval)*

721 Tank *(K. J. Choi)*

722 Woosie *(Ian Woosnam)*

723
The Babe
(Mildred Didrickson Zaharias)

745
The Emperor
(Bobby Jones)

The Future Mrs. Sturgis

The story which I am about to tell begins in what might be called the middle period of Sturgis's career. He had reached the stage when his handicap was a wobbly twelve; and, as you are no doubt aware, it is then that a man really begins to golf in the true sense of the word. Mortimer's fondness for the game until then had been merely tepid compared with what it became now. He had played a little before, but now

HERE'S TO YOU, MY VALENTINE

he really buckled to and got down to it. It was at this point, too, that he began once more to entertain thoughts of marriage. A profound statistician in this one department, he had discovered that practically all the finest exponents of the art are married men; and the thought that there might be something in the holy state which improved a man's game, and that he was missing a good thing, troubled him a great deal. Moreover, the paternal instinct had

> he had reached the stage when his handicap was a wobbly twelve; and, as you are no doubt aware, it is then that a man really begins to golf in the true sense of the word.

awakened in him. As he justly pointed out, whether marriage improved our game or not, it was to Old Tom Morris's marriage that the existence of young Tommy Morris, winner of the British Open Championship four times in succession, could be directly traced. In fact, at the age of forty-two, Mortimer Sturgis was in just the frame of mind to take some nice girl aside and ask her to become a step-mother to his eleven drivers, his baffy, his twenty-eight putters, and the rest of the ninety-four clubs which he had accumulated in the course of his golfing career. The sole stipulation, of course, which he made when dreaming his day-dreams, was that the future Mrs. Sturgis must be a golfer. I can still recall the horror in his face when one girl, admirable in other respects, said that she had never heard of Harry Vardon, and didn't he mean Dolly Vardon? She has since proved an excellent wife and mother, but Mortimer Sturgis never spoke to her again.

P.G. Wodehouse
Sundered Hearts

746
Sharing the love
of golf with
someone special

747
A mixed
foursome

748
Going on a golf date

749
Watching your
girlfriend sink an 8-foo
putt to win the hole

750

Husbands and wives can play golf together

Golf is like a love affair:
If you don't take it seriously, it's not
fun; if you do take it seriously, it
breaks your heart.

Arnold Daly

GOLF
FASHION

Even if you can't play like a pro,
you can still dress like one.

751
The cashmere argyle sweater you got
for Father's Day ten years ago

752
An old Panama hat that fits perfectly
after years of wear and doesn't
blow off in a wind

753
Traditional black FootJoys

754
Pastel polyester Sans-a-Belt slacks

755
Golf shoes with kilties

756
A hat that makes
you feel like
Ben Hogan

761
Being in the best-dressed
foursome at the
club tournament

758
A V-neck golf
sweater from
Pebble Beach

760
A stylish
golf cardigan

757
Plus-fours and
argyle socks

759
Smart shoes

The Well-Dressed Golfer

I will say for Perkins that when he decided to commit to golf he went about it in a very thorough manner. He had himself surveyed for three knickerbocker suits, he laid in a stock of soft shirts, imported stockings and spiked shoes, and he gave our professional carte blanche in the matter of field equipment. It is not a safe thing to give a Scotchman permission to dip his hand in your change pocket, and MacPherson certainly availed himself of the opportunity to finger some of the Dubuque money. He took one look at the novice and unloaded on him something less than a hundredweight of dead stock. He also gave him a lesson or two, and sent him forth armed to the teeth with wood, iron and aluminum.

Charles E. Van Loan
The Ooley Cow, 1918

770 Lucky shoes

771 Walter Hagen's sartorial splendor

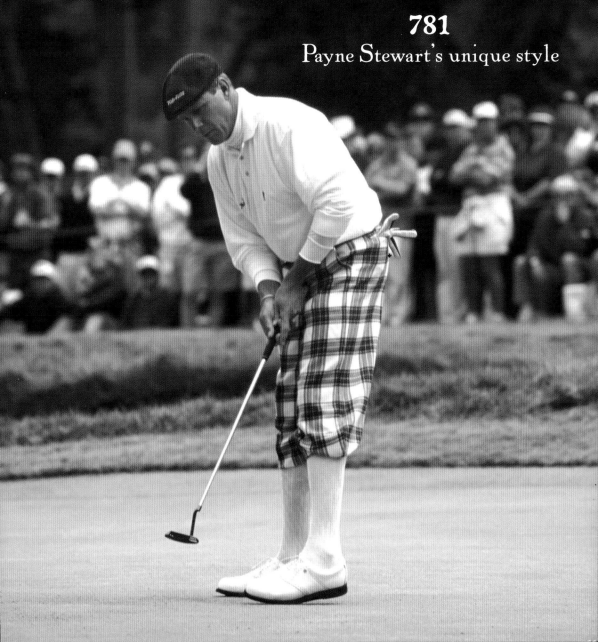

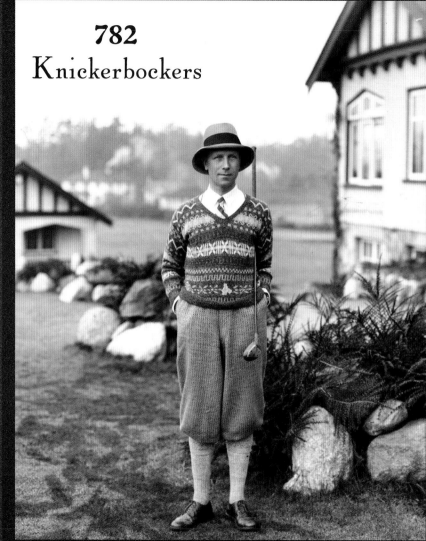

782

Knickerbockers

A Question of Knickerbockers

The burning question which divides golfers into two hostile camps is the choice between knickerbockers and trousers ... To a man with a really well-turned calf and neat ankles I should say, wear knickerbockers whenever you get a chance. The late Lord Septimus Boulger, who had very thick legs and calves that seemed to begin just above the ankles, used to wear knickerbockers because he said it put his opponent off his play.

Golf and Good form,
from *Mr. Punch's Golf Stories*

Golf Fashion Advice: 1902

The most popular style of costume during the summer months is a cotton shirt-waist with a short skirt of white duck or piqué, but personally I do not like this color, because I have found it has a tendency to make me take my eye off the ball, particularly in putting, and for this reason I think a broadcloth, tailor-made skirt of any other color than white is the best to play in.

Genevieve Hecker
Golf for Women

783
Finding just the right golf outfit

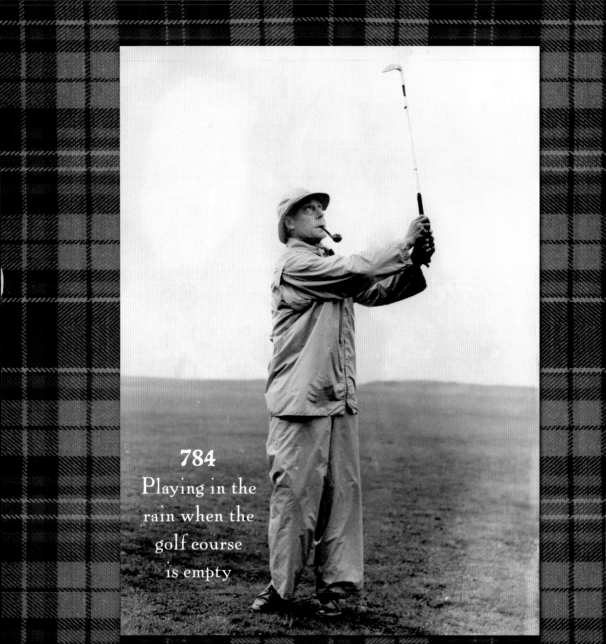

784
Playing in the
rain when the
golf course
is empty

785
Breaking 100 for the first time

786
Remembering a swing tip that always works

787
Clearing a tall tree with a 100-yard wedge shot

788
Putting out of a greenside sand trap

789
Breaking 90 for the first time

790
Assistant pros and bartenders who listen while
you go over your round stroke by stroke,
primarily because they can't leave

791
"Fluff"
Mike Cowan
accompanied
Tiger
in his
early tour
victories

LEGENDARY CADDIES

*Part craftsman, part adviser and part companion,
caddies carry much more than golf bags on their shoulders.*

792
Al "Rabbit" Dyer

Caddied for Gary Player for 18 years

793
Angelo Argea

Toted Jack Nicklaus's bag for almost two decades

794
Carl Jackson

Ben Crenshaw's caddie at both of his Masters victories

795
Daw Anderson

Caddied for Alan Robertson

796
Eddie Lowery

*The 10-year-old caddie who carried Francis Ouimet's
bag when he won the Open*

797 Fanny Sunesson, Nick Faldo's long time bag-toting partner

798 Freddie Bennett, caddie master at Augusta National for 40 years

799 Ernest "Creamy" Carolan, Arnold Palmer's caddie

800 Herman Mitchell, long time caddie for Lee Trevino

801 James "Tip" Anderson, St. Andrews legendary caddie and Arnold Palmer's caddie in the British Open

Fanny Sunesson with Nick Faldo at the 2002 U.S. Op

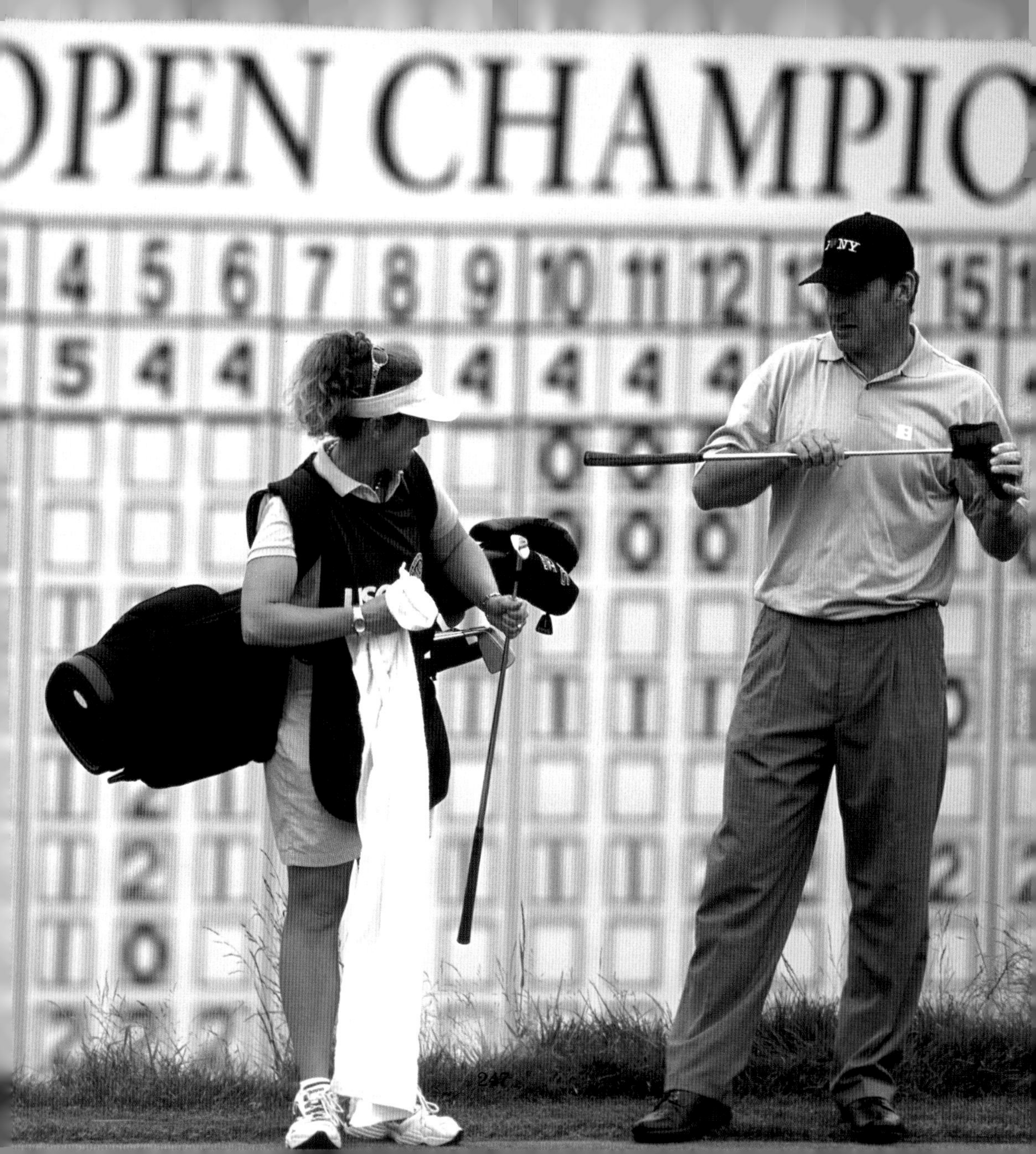
OPEN CHAMPIO

802
Fond memories of summers
caddying at the local golf course

803 Jim Clark, still worked at Baltusrol at the age of 90

804 Lee Lynch, caddied for Al Geiberger when he shot his record round of 59

805 Kirky, caddy to Tom Morris

806 Lorne "Rabbit" LeBere, longtime PGA and Senior PGA tour caddie

807 Steve Williams, Tiger Woods's star caddie

808 Ross "Cotton" Young, caddie at Saucon Valley Country Club for over 71 years

809 Sam "Killer" Foy worked for Hale Irwin and Jack Nicklaus (45 years on the Tour)

810 Willie Peterson, Jack Nicklaus's caddie at Augusta

THEY CA ME "BREEKS" BUT MY MAIDEN NAMES McINTOSH

811
Francis Ouimet

The 20-year-old
caddie who won the
1913 U.S. Open,
beating Harry Vardon
by five strokes in an 18
hole play-off

Francis Ouimet

In Ouimet, the first amateur to win the U.S. Open, America at last had its own bona fide golf hero, a soft-spoken, self-effacing young man who, despite coming from modest means, had all the marks of a gentleman. He didn't drink, he didn't boast, he didn't cuss as many of the amateurs and most of the pros did. And there was a gentleness about Francis that endeared him to all.

While being paraded around Brookline on the shoulders of the delirious fans, he leaned over to speak to a small woman, "Thank you, Mother," he said. "I'll be home soon."

George Peper
The Story of Golf

812
The legendary caddies
of St. Andrews

A Man of Few Words

"FIERY"

The old-fashioned Scottish caddie will soon be as extinct as the dodo, and we have great pleasure, therefore, in giving a portrait of James Carey, one of the few surviving members of the tribe. Carey, or, as he is universally known to golfers, "Fiery," is a native of Musselburgh and is now fifty-four years of age. He has spent all his life in the service of golf and golfers and was at one time an excellent player. He was a favourite caddie of the late Mr. John Blackwood, the publisher, and he has officiated in important matches in the same capacity for young Tom Morris, Bob Ferguson, and most of the famous players of the past generation—amateur and professional. He now invariably carries for Willie Park, Jr., and he has become a familiar figure at championship times at Sandwich and Hoylake. "Fiery" is a man of few words, and his quaint physiognomy and blue bonnet, which no living eye has ever seen him remove, render him an object of the greatest interest to the young English caddies, who regard him with mingled respect and dread. In reality Carey is a most amiable man and a great favourite with his employers.

Garden G. Smith
Golfing Notes,
The Tatler
October 23, 1901

Observing your partner's swing ritual

Alexander Paterson has always been a careful rather than a dashing player. It is his custom, a sort of ritual, to take **two measured practice swings** before addressing the ball, even on the putting green. When he does address the ball **he shuffles his feet** for a moment or two, then pauses, and **scans the horizon in a suspicious sort of way,** as if he had been expecting it to play some sort of a trick on him when he was not looking. A careful inspection seems to convince him of the horizon's bona fides, and he turns his attention to the ball again. He **shuffles his feet** once more, then raises his club. He **waggles the club smartly** over the ball three times, then lays it behind the globule. At this point he suddenly **peers at the horizon again**, in the apparent hope of catching it off its guard. This done, he **raises his club very slowly, brings it back very slowly** till it almost touches the ball, **raises it again,** brings it down again, **raises it once more,** and **brings it down for the third time.** He then stands motionless, wrapped in thought, like some Indian fakir contemplating the infinite. Then he **raises his club again** and replaces it behind the ball. Finally he **quivers all over**, swings very slowly back, and **drives the ball** for about a hundred and fifty yards in a dead straight line.

P.G. Wodehouse
Ordeal by Golf

GOLF NUMBER

Life

PRICE 10 CENTS
Vol. 64, No. 1662. September 3, 1914
Copyright, 1914, Life Publishing Company

814
A jumbo bucket of
range balls for $3.00

815
A new, cushy mat at the driving range

816
Video taping your swing

817
The smell of driving range hot dogs

818
Hitting the 200-yard sign on the fly

819
The small pyramids of
practice balls at fancy resorts

820

A summer
evening at
the driving
range

THROUGH REPETITION THE MAGIC
WILL BE FORCED TO RISE.

ALCHEMICAL PRECEPT

What happens at the range is simpler and sometimes more therapeutic than golf: You buy a bucket of worn-out balls and then pound the daylights out of them. Some of us do this in the hope that by accident or mere repetition we might reform our swings. Some of us have much deeper troubles.

Charles McGrath
Swingin' in the Rain

All golfers, men and women, professional and amateur, are united by one thing— their desire to improve.

Judy Rankin

831 Chipping in the backyard on a late summer evening

832 Doing air swings in front of a mirror

833 Installing a putting green in your own backyard

834 Hitting a bucket of balls on the way home from work

835 Chipping on the hotel room carpet

836 Putting into a glass on the living room carpet

837 Swinging an umbrella in the office

838 Spending an hour on the chipping green perfecting your short game

839 Setting up a practice net in the backyard

840 A dollar-a-hole skins putting game with a bunch of friends

Practicing is my meditation.
Some golfers like to fish
and others like to read.
I like to hit golf balls.

Lee Trevino

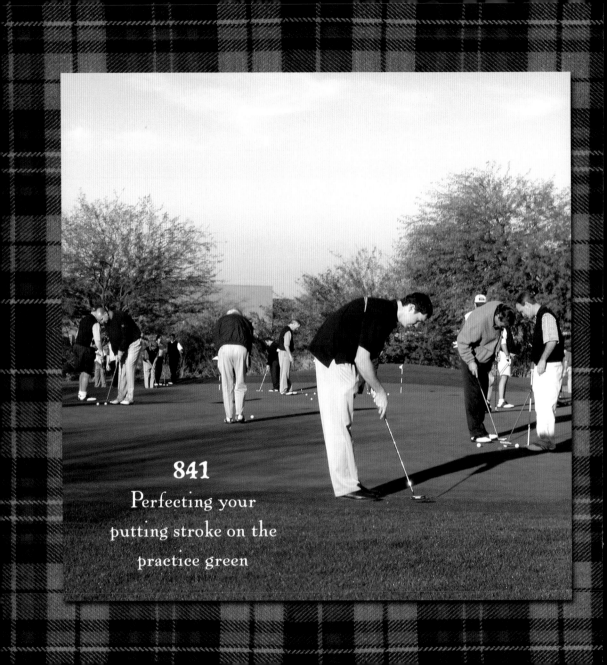

841
Perfecting your
putting stroke on the
practice green

"A non-smoking single for a right-handed golfer, please."

Not every hotel or motel room is ideally suited to golf. In most rooms, there's a big window (with the requisite heavy curtains) at one end, a big bed or two on one side, and a bureau, desk, and so forth on the other side. If you are a right-handed golfer and the beds are on the left as you face the window, you have plenty of room to take a full swing without unduly damaging furniture. If the beds are on the right, however, you run the risk of smashing the TV at the top of your backswing. In such a room, a golfer is limited to putts, chips, and three-quarter knockdown shots. The wisest course is probably to specify the type of room you need when you make your reservation: "I'd like a non-smoking single for a right-handed golfer, please." Of course, the ideal room also has a big mirror on the wall over the bureau, so that you can stand on your bed and check your takeaway from three different angles. The mattress makes any weight shift errors instantly obvious, but only in the older, more luxurious hotels—those with high ceilings—is it possible to take a full swing while standing on the bed.

David Owen
My Usual Game

842
The first time out
with a new driver

GOLF CLUBS WE LOVE

*Technology keeps improving and styles continue to change,
but from time to time a club distinguishes itself and
achieves a place on the exclusive list of
"classics and trendsetters."*

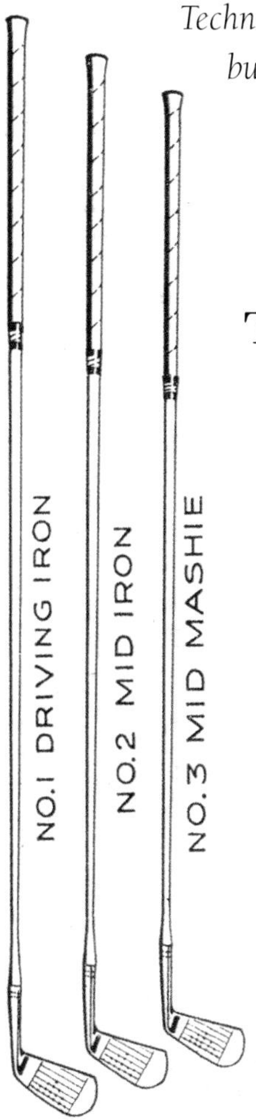

843

The Troon Clubs, the oldest known set of
golf clubs in the world

844

The Schenectady putter

845

The Auchterlonie brassey

846

Hugh Philp's long-nose driving club

847

Bobby Jones's Calamity Jane putter

848

Alan Shepard's telescoping
6-iron moon club

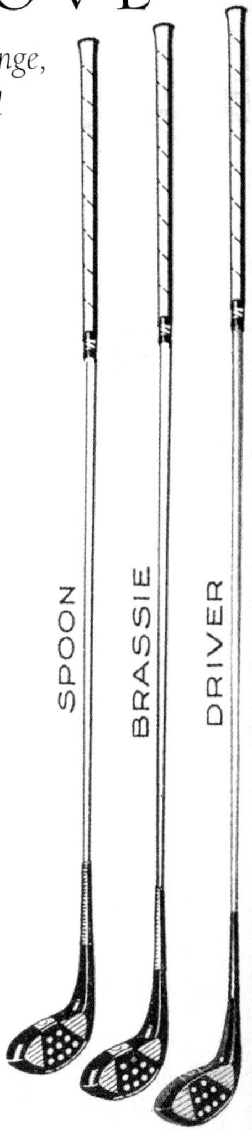

NO.1 DRIVING IRON

NO.2 MID IRON

NO.3 MID MASHIE

SPOON

BRASSIE

DRIVER

Sean Arnold's
Sports Antiquities
shop in London

849
The evolution of
the golf club

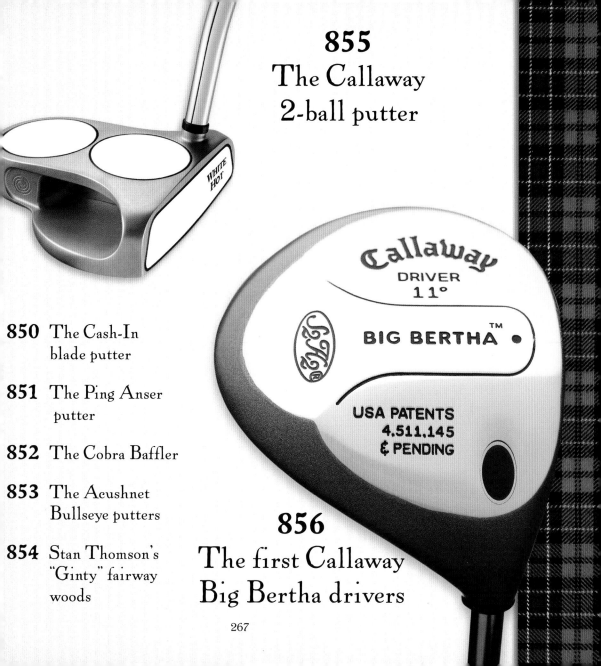

855
The Callaway
2-ball putter

WHITE HOT

Callaway
DRIVER
11°

BIG BERTHA™ •

USA PATENTS
4.511.145
& PENDING

856
The first Callaway
Big Bertha drivers

857
Shopping for a
new driver

A golf shop in St. Andrews

A Question of Balance

ill a glass tumbler or a cup with hot tap water until several inches deep. For every inch of water, add one to two tablespoons of Epsom salt. Add salt until a test ball floats, with the top of the ball just above the water line. Add one drop of Jet-Dri dishwasher despotting agent to reduce the surface tension (friction) of the water; the balls will then spin more freely in the solution.

Test one ball at a time. Don't just drop the ball in; spin it in the solution between your thumb and forefinger. The ball will rotate for several seconds, gradually slowing to a stop. Notice how the ball comes to a stop. If it comes to a gradual stop without any rocking motion, put a dot on top with a felt-tip permanent marker. Now spin it again. If it comes to a halt again without rocking and stops with a different area on top (i.e., anywhere but the spot you marked), you have a balanced ball (one with no heavy or light side). Remove the ball, dry it off, and put a second dot right next to the first one. The two dots signify a perfectly balanced ball. Save these balls for a tournament or a big match. They will give you some extra confidence for your crucial putts.

Most of the balls you test will slow down, then rock back and forth before coming to a stop. This rocking motion occurs when the ball's heavy side is settling toward the bottom of the container. The part that settles above the surface is the light side; place a single dot at the very center of the light side. As you test balls you will get a feeling for the severity of the rocking motion. Keep balls that don't rock too much for important rounds. When you mark and replace your ball on the green, place it with the light side (the dot) up so that the heavy and light side will roll end over end, and your putt's line of roll won't be affected.

Dave Pelz
Putt Like the Pros

The Spalding Kro-Flite

The Uniroyal Plus Six

The Spalding Dot

The Dunlop 65

The Flying Lady

The Golden Ram

The Titleist Pro-V1

The Maxfli Noodle

The Callaway Rule 35

The Spalding Top-Flite

The Titleist Tour Balata

GOLF BALLS

During a single round, a golf ball is subjected to repeated blows
and various curses. It is never sure of its destiny, until it rests peacefully
at the bottom of a pond or is sentenced to the driving range for life.
Yet, its independent spirit deserves the respect and admiration of all.

871
In the beginning there was the
wooden golf ball

872
The featherie

873
The gutta percha ball

874
The Bramble

875
The Haskell ball

876
The Vardon Flyer

877
Finding a brand new Titleist
in the short rough

878
The Penfold Ace

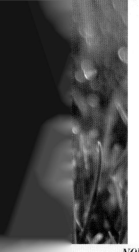

NOW
SPALDING
GOLF BALLS STAY WHITE
resist scuffing, bruises
and stains

LIFETIME WHITE
A spectacular permanent whiteness

Now to distance, Spalding adds dazzle. To the Dot's sweet feel, click, and absolute uniformity, Spalding adds a big new plus: permanent whiteness.

Spalding *Lifetime White* is the whitest, brightest white, the toughest, highest gloss white of any ball you ever played. Resists scuffing, bruises, stains ... won't yellow or chip.

THEY'RE ALL LIFETIME WHITE

The Dot, golf's greatest ball. Tru-Tension wound. The perfect companion for power hitters. The Top-Flite, distance plus toughness. The Par-Flite, Tru-Flite and other fine Spalding balls.

SPALDING DOT, TOP-FLITE, PAR-FLITE, TRU-FLITE sold through golf professionals only.

COLLECTING
GOLF THINGS

*A game as complex and rich with details is bound to
inspire some serious collecting. These are some
examples of the treasures we love to accumulate.*

887
Discovering a set of dusty old hickory-shafted
clubs in the back of an antiques store

888
A collection of bag tags from the
best courses around the world

889
Antique golf balls and boxes

890
Buying golf memorabilia on the internet

891
Old English cigarette cards
with golfing characters

892
Autographed golf balls and flags

893 Collecting old golf clubs

Not for want of clubs

I t was not for want of clubs that Mr. Polwinkle's handicap obstinately refused to fall below sixteen. His rack full of them extended round three sides of the smoking room. In addition, there was an enormous box resembling a sarcophagus on the floor, and in one corner was a large loose heap of clubs. To get one out of the heap without sending the others crashing to the ground was as delicate and difficult as a game of spillikins, and the housemaid had bestowed on it many an early morning malediction.

The rack along one side of the wall was clearly of a peculiarly sacred character. The clips holding the clubs were of plush, and behind each clip there was pasted on the wall an inscription in Mr. Polwinkle's meticulously neat handwriting. There was a driver stated to have belonged to the great James Braid; a mashie of J.H. Taylor's; a spoon of Herd's...

Mr. Polwinkle tried to soothe himself by looking at his treasures. Ah! If only he could just for one day be endued with the slash and power of those who had played with them.

Bernard Darwin
The Wooden Putter

MEDINAH
COUNTRY CLUB
No. 2 Course

DATE						W.+ L.− H.O
YARDS	Ladies Par	Par Men's		HDCP	HOLE	
400L 390S	4	4	6	1	
414	4	5	7	2	
130	3	3	18	3	
290L 277S		4	14	4	
315L 304S		4	12	5	
155L 146S	3	3	16	6	
576L 516S	5	6	1	7	
425	4	5	5	8	
445L 433S	4	5	4	9	
3150	35	39		OUT	64

314L 267S	4	4	13	10	
396L 387S	4	4	8	11	
336L 323S		4	11	12	
485	5	5	2	13	
332	4	4	10	14	
189L 180S		3	17	15	
483L 468S	5	5	3	16	
174L 159S	3	3	15	17	
344L 326S		4	9	18	
3053	36	36		IN	
6203	71	75		OUT	
				TOTAL	
				HANDICAP	
				NET SCORE	

SCORER

PLAYER'S CIGARETTES

1 TOP OF SWING

A. G. Beck

2 IMPACT

No. 4
SH

Note fairly straight left arm in ba
slightly in advance of club-he

WILLS'S CIGARETTES

PLAYER'S CIGARETTES

POND

ROUGH GRASS

ROUGH
GRASS

POND

CLUB HOUSE ROAD
HONOURABLE COMPANY
OF EDINBURGH GOLFERS, MUIRFIELD

ALWAYS WINNING

© REINTHAL & NEWMAN, PUBS., N.Y.

908 A collection of treasured golf hats

909 Old canvas golf bags with worn brown leather trim

910 Saving old scorecards from memorable rounds

904 Interesting clubmakers' stamps on old irons and putters

905 Persimmon woods with brass plates and intricate Cycolac inserts

906 A visit to Sean Arnold's fascinating golf antiquities shop in London's Notting Hill

907 Albums of old photos from golf vacations

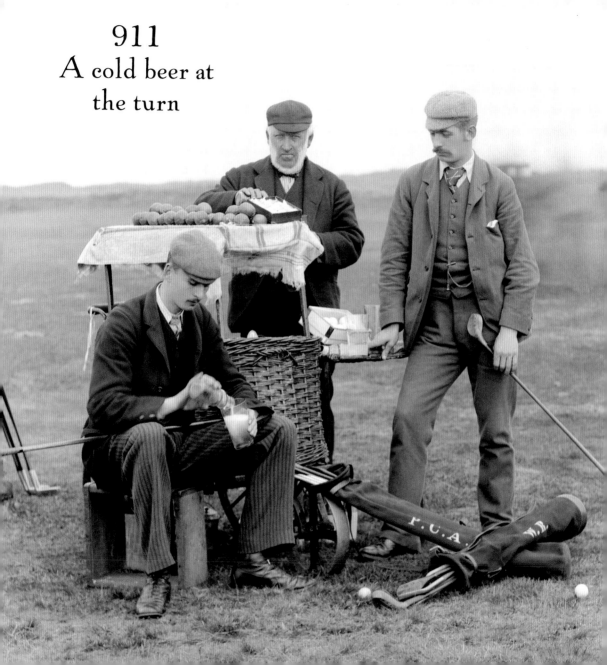

911
A cold beer at
the turn

DINING ON THE LINKS

The game's spirit of camaraderie displays itself in many ways, including well-established dining and drinking traditions. From basic hot dogs to Augusta's famed pimento sandwiches, golfers enjoy a wide choice of culinary delights to comfort themselves during and after the battle against par.

912 Cheeseburgers, chicken salad, and tuna salad, three things every club chef knows how to prepare

913 Reliable club sandwiches on white toast

914 The half-way house

915 Discussing your round with friends at the 19th hole

916 Clam chowder on the course on a chilly day at Pine Lakes in Myrtle Beach

917 Pimento cheese sandwiches at The Masters, preferably eaten under a tree at Amen Corner

918 A cold Budweiser to help lubricate the swing

919 Sharing the dining table at Prestwick, where you wear a necktie even at lunch and always sit next to someone

920 A hot cup of coffee before teeing off on a chilly April morning

921 A seafood dinner at a Myrtle Beach restaurant

922 A silver flask of whiskey for a cold day on the links

923 An energy-boosting Snickers bar

924 An Irish pub with golf prints on the wall

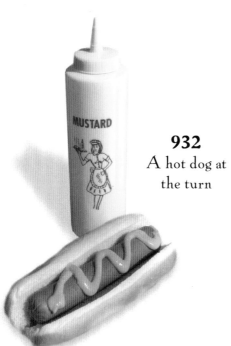

932
A hot dog at the turn

925 Cocktails at sunset beneath the lighthouse at the Harbour Town yacht basin in Hilton Head, a tee shot away from the 18th green

926 A glass of Callaway Chardonnay or Greg Norman Shiraz

927 Hot chocolate at the turn on a cool October day

928 Peach cobbler at Augusta National (available only in the clubhouse)

929 A frosted mug of cold beer in hand while sitting on the terrace overlooking the 18th green

930 Stopping in a nearby pub after round in Scotland

931 *Tee Time at the Masters*, the classic golf cookbook

933 The all-you-can-eat buffet dinner after the local golf tournament

934 The arrival of the beverage cart on the horizon

935 The Champions Dinner at The Masters

936 The food-ordering phone by the 8th tee

937 "The Sand Wedge" sandwich on almost every clubhouse lunch menu

938 Sitting around the living room with golf buddies eating potato chips and watching the last day of the U.S. Open

939 Bringing a picnic lunch to a big tournament

940 Buying your daughter an ice cream cone on her first trip to the driving range

The ideal grillroom makes no distinction between men and women, but women tend to prefer the outdoor patio that overlooks the ninth or eighteenth hole. Inside, there is a television that is always turned to golf whenever golf is on, and the guy who switches it to baseball in July gets the bowl of peanuts thrown at him.

Jerry Tarde
What Makes the Ideal Clubhouse—and Club?

THE STUFF
OF GOLF

*The neverending search for a magic piece of equipment
is part of what makes the game so much fun. Neither
economics nor rationality play a major role.*

941
Golf pencils, golf towels, bag tags, pitch forks,
ball markers, yardage books, scorecards,
and a pocket full of wooden tees:
the necessary tools of golf

942
The care we take with a new set of irons

943
The feel of new grips

944
Inspecting each others' drivers during the first
tee wait; holding them up, putting them down,
not really knowing what we're looking for

945
A bench with a view of the course

946 Animal head covers

947

Yardage markers

Catalog No. CR245

COMBINATION MAT

COMPLETELY NEW WEAVE COMBINATION MAT PRECISION MADE. Heavy duty full 1" thick airplane tire carcasses—reinforced with NYLON CORD FABRIC, WELDED ENDS, heavy gauge galvanized spring steel wire, NO CLIPS TO BREAK.

NEW WEAVE ALLOWS you to place the RUBBER TEE ANYWHERE in the MAT, NO HOLES NEED TO BE CUT.

O GOLF BALL MARKER
es full name in one line. In-
ink and 3 letters of each, A-Z.

948 Bunker rakes, hole cutters, mowers, turf aerators, and sprinkler heads

949 Flagsticks and flags

950 Signature tee markers and hole signs

951 Hi-tech double-strap stand bags

952 12-foot long ball retrievers

953 Bag stands, pull carts, wooden lockers, and shoe cleaners

954 Shag bags and ball shaggers

955 Golf carts with GPS

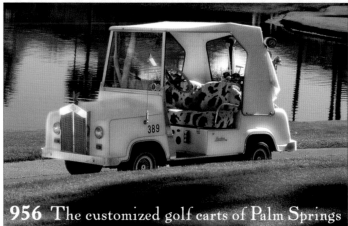

956 The customized golf carts of Palm Springs

957
Lucky balls, water balls, and smilers

958
The feel of a new golf glove

959
Hand-knit headcovers with pompoms

960
Leather clubhead covers with
appliquéd numbers

961
A small plastic clicker to keep track
of your score

962
Pro bags

963
Monogrammed golf tees

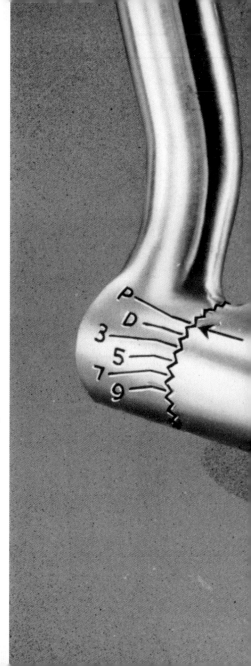

973
Byron Nelson's incredible
1945 streak of victories

SIGNATURES

Some things we love about our favorite players.

❧

974
Bobby Jones's unassuming heroism

975
Jack Nicklaus's determination

976
Ben Hogan's secret

977
Walter Hagen's dashing style

978
Sam Snead's signature hat

979
Fred Couples's easy swing

980
Old Tom Morris's pioneer spirit

981 Annika Sorenstam's brilliant 59

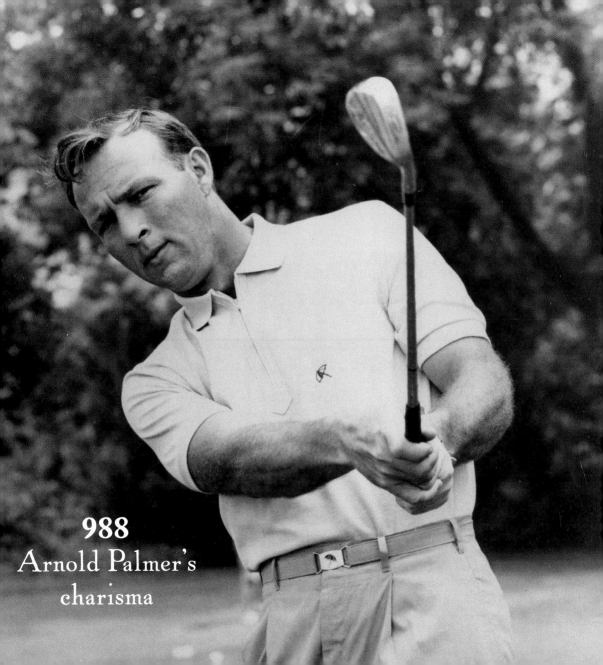

988
Arnold Palmer's
charisma

989
Johnny Miller's laser-like
iron game

990
Payne Stewart's
emotional victories

991
Doug Sanders's yellow,
pink and green clothes

992
Seve Ballesteros's
daring recoveries

993
Ben Crenshaw's love of the
game's traditions

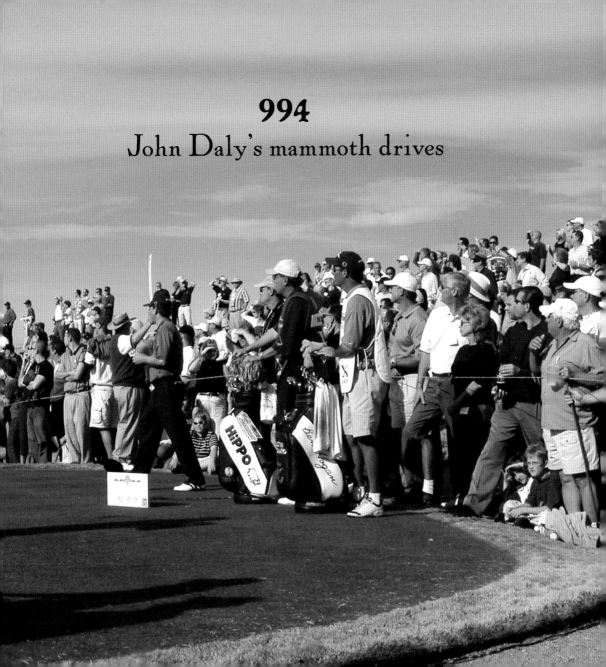

994
John Daly's mammoth drives

995
A crisp pitching wedge shot to an elevated green

What other sport offers
such sudden splendor
in exchange for so few
calories of expended energy?
In those instants of whiz,
ascent, hover, and fall,
an ideal self seems
mirrored.

John Updike

996
Golf inspires us
to try things we thought
we could never do

997

Golf is the triumph of hope

over experience.

998
Dennis Walters, and his assistant, Benji Hogan

never give up your dream

Dennis Walters always wanted to be a professional golfer. His dreams were shattered 25 years ago, when as the result of an accident, he found himself paralyzed from the waist down. Today however, Dennis is once again busy fulfilling his lifetime dream. Tightly secured by a safety belt to his specially-designed golf cart, Dennis entertains and delights the crowds with an amazing repertoire of "specialty" shots. For those of us who have trouble with our drives, watching Dennis hit a ball 260 yards down the middle of the fairway with a rubber-hose shafted driver is an enlightening experience. His message: never give up your dream. He is proof that hard work, perseverance and the love of golf can overcome considerable hardship.

INSPIRATION

Adversity has never stopped a man with golf in his veins.
Some have even transcended their physical limitations
and become inspirations for us all.

🏌

rnest Jones, one of the game's great early
teachers, lost a leg below the knee during
World War I. He stayed in the hospital four
months. The day after leaving he shot a one-legged
round of 83. Despite his handicap Jones was so
dextrous with a golf club that he could sit in a chair
and drive a ball two hundred yards. Another veteran
of World War I was Tommy Armour, who served in
the British tank corps and nearly lost his sight in
one eye during a battle. Armour went on to win the
U.S. Open, the PGA, and the British Open playing
with metal plates in his arm and head.

Kevin Nelson
The Greatest Golf Shot Ever Made

A future full of possibilities

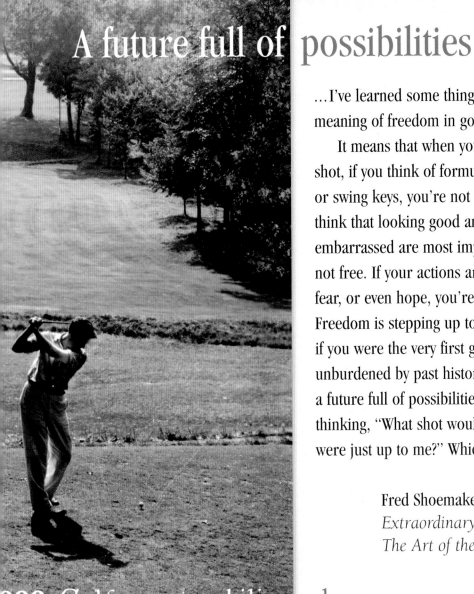

...I've learned some things about the meaning of freedom in golf.

It means that when you step up to a shot, if you think of formulas, checklists, or swing keys, you're not free. If you think that looking good and not being embarrassed are most important, you're not free. If your actions are shaped by fear, or even hope, you're not free. Freedom is stepping up to a shot as if you were the very first golfer, unburdened by past history, with a future full of possibilities. Freedom is thinking, "What shot would I hit if it were just up to me?" Which it is.

Fred Shoemaker
Extraordinary Golf:
The Art of the Possible

999 Golf tests our ability to let go

The 15th hole at the Francis H. I'i Brown Golf
Course (South Course) at the Mauna Lani Resort,
Kohala Coast, Island of Hawaii

The Sixth Principle:
Play One Shot at a Time

Only one golf swing can take place at one moment in time. Just as a journey is comprised of singular moments, so is a round of golf comprised of single shots. If you focus on the past or worry about the future, you cannot be in the present. Let go of that double bogey on the last hole, don't stress about the water on the next. Focus solely on the shot in front of you—that is the only way you'll have any chance of success. This is what makes golf such a great metaphor for life. Live your life, moment by moment. And with golf, play it one shot at a time.

Darrin Gee
Founder and Senior Coach,
Ke'ano Kolepa – The Spirit of Golf

The Simple Delights of the Game

But may not also the simple delights of the game and its surroundings, with their effect upon the mind and the emotions, be included under the allurements and the mystery of golf? My knowledge of links up to the present is limited, but on mine there are delights which, to me a duffer, are like Pisgah sights: **hills, valleys, trees, a gleaming lake in the distance**, a grand and beloved piece of bunting lending gorgeous colour to the scene; **a hospitable club-house with spacious verandas and arm-chairs**; shower-baths; tea and toast; whisky and soda; genial companionship; and the ever-delectable pipe. Has anyone yet sung these delights of the game? The **comradeship in sport**, the friendliness, the community of sentiment, the frankness of speech, the goodwill, the "generosity in trifles"? Or of the links

themselves? **The great breeze that greets you on the hill**, the whiffs of air—pungent, penetrating—that come through green things growing, the **hot smell of pines at noon**, the wet smell of fallen leaves in autumn, the damp and heavy air of the valleys at eve, the lungs full of oxygen, **the sense of freedom on a great expanse**, the exhilaration, the vastness, the buoyancy, the exaltation? . . . And how beautiful the vacated links at dawn, when dew gleams untrodden beneath the pendant flags and the

long shadows lie quiet on the green; when no caddie intrudes upon the still and silent lawns, and you stroll from hole to hole and **drink in the beauties of a land** to which you know you will be all to blind when the sun mounts high and you toss for the honour!

Arnold Haultain

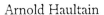
The Mystery of Golf

The game itself is a kind of narrative.
We set off, full of hope and expectation,
we encounter difficulties and reversals, our character
is tested, our spirits soar and plummet, and then we
head for home, where, with relief or sadness, or
maybe both, we rap the final putt into its hole.
Then, as soon as we're done, we play it all over again
in our heads, and it gets better and better
in the telling and retelling.

Charles McGrath and David McCormick
The Ultimate Golf Book

1001
A lifetime full of golfing memories

Putting together this book was a rich and wonderful journey, but one that we did not take alone. We are grateful to so many people for helping us fulfill our dream. First, we would like to thank Leslie Stoker, our publisher, (a non-golfer) who believed early on that there were at least 1,001 reasons to love golf. We give thanks to calm, cool and collected Beth Huseman who guided us with humor, patience and occasional chocolates, and to everyone at Stewart, Tabori & Chang who were willing to work on this massive undertaking.

Our book was enriched beyond words by the wisdom of sports writer Ron Green, who added spirit and substance, along with some really great details. His son (and our good golf friend), Dave Green, shared ideas and provided moral support during our darkest hours.

Enormous gratitude goes out to Saundra Sheffer, formerly of the Ralph Miller Golf Library, who edited our list and kept us on track. Her knowledge of the game and its history were invaluable and her sense of humor delightful!

So many people helped to make this a visually rich and interesting book. Maxine Vigliotta, Rand Jerris and everyone at the USGA Photographic Archives in Far Hills, New Jersey were amazing in their patience and professionalism. Their library became a home away from home for a few magical months. Cilla Jackson of St. Andrews University Library helped us navigate through their vast collection of golf imagery. Wayne Wilson at the Amateur Athletic League in Los Angeles helped us through our eleventh hour requests with grace.

Many wonderful courses shared their photographs with us, and special thanks go out to Tim Greenwell and Cyndi Bush of Troon Golf; Marla Taylor of Bandon Dunes Resort; Ann Reineking of Whistling Straits, Kohler, Wisconsin; everyone at The Boulders Resort; Ashley Allen of Wild Wing Plantation in Myrtle Beach; Stephanie Reid of The Princeville Resort; the great people at Callaway Golf; Matt Keppler and Bruce Harmon of Bruce Harmon School of Golf; Steve Wheeler and everyone at the beautiful Coeur d'Alene Resort in pristine Idaho. To Kenny

Rankin, Michael Douglas and Catherine Zeta-Jones for graciously providing pictures, we thank you. And mahalo to Darrin Gee and Darien Hsu Gee of Ke'ano Kolepa —The Spirit of Golf, for providing us not only with images but with vision and enthusiasm just when we needed it!

Thanks go out to Carl Mickelson and Dave Pelz of Dave Pelz Golf for believing in our project, to Dennis Walters for providing inspiration, and to Rob Myers of the Phoenix Open for allowing us to photograph their great tournament.

To George and Libby Peper, George and Susan Lewis of Golfiana, Leo Kelly, Sean Arnold, Marty Hackle and Barry Hyde we thank you for your friendship and golf wisdom.

To our golfing friends and family who contributed their thoughts and reasons over the course of this book —John Elliott, Craig Marson, the Pedroli family, Nick Ludington, Arthur Feola, David Englander, Bernie Doyle, Roger Hooker, Jim Harrison, Mark Morris, Joe Hyde, Don Reilly, Dianna Russo, Eric Glaser, Diana Catherines, Bob and Tricia Irish, Dave and Mandy Jones, Carrie and John Shipley, Sue and Bernie Smith, Dan O'Connell and all the Griffins—we wish you the very best that golf can offer. And to our non-golfing friends—Milbry Polk and Leila Hadley Luce who replenished our golf collection, Ahleyah Aberer, Robin Siegel, Jimmy Webb, Chris Miele, Melinda Barber and Tom Ritchie, Kim Moreton, Roger Pring, Tim and Norma Jenns, Jana Kolpen, and Muriel Allen—we thank you for your support and understanding of our obsession.

And to Janet O'Meara whose love of the game inspired all around her. Thank you one and all.

Hubert Pedroli & Mary Tiegreen

We would like to thank the following individuals and groups for granting us the right to publish their words and images. All efforts have been made to identify the copyright holders of materials in this book, and we apologize for any errors. Please contact us through our publisher with additions or corrections.

Text credits: Extracts from P.G. Wodehouse, pages 24, 67, 226, 254: Courtesy of the Trustees of the Wodehouse Estate ⁓ 84: Courtesy of Golf Digest and John Updike ⁓ 270 Courtesy of HarperCollins

Image credits: Pages 2, 36, 45, 65, 70, 134, 158, 191, 194, 201, 211, 217, 222, 295, 299, 304 Courtesy of the USGA. All rights reserved; 98, 100, 216, 237, 247 © USGA/John Mummert; 28, 72, 97, 102, 298 © USGA/Robert Walker; 198 © USGA/Phil Arnold; 99, 101, 244 © USGA/J.D. Cuban ⁓ 128, 133, 154-5, 252, 268, 284 Courtesy of St. Andrews University Library Photographic Collection ⁓ 8, 80, 90, 126, 186, 220, 248, 250, 310 Courtesy of the Library of Congress ⁓ 189 Courtesy of NASA ⁓ 236 Courtesy of The Amateur Athletic Foundation ⁓ 50, 82, 108, 109, 110, 112, 116, 146, 148, 149, 161, 170, 171, 173, 180, 234, 235, 256, 257, 262, 266, 271, 272, 274, 275, 278, 286, 287, 289, 290, 291, 292, 294, 301 photographs © Mary Tiegreen ⁓ 243, 276 photographs © Hubert Pedroli ⁓ 10, 14, 16, 21, 23, 25, 49, 51, 57, 58, 66, 68, 69, 74, 76, 81, 84, 87, 104, 107, 118, 122, 123, 124, 125, 127, 129, 136, 139, 142, 144, 150, 160, 162, 164, 167, 175, 176, 178, 204, 207, 208, 226, 228, 230, 232, 238, 240, 241, 242, 246, 249, 253, 255, 258, 260, 261, 263, 264, 265, 269, 280, 281, 282, 283, 291, 296, 302, 306 from the Tiegreen/Pedroli Golf Ephemera Collection ⁓ 32, 46, 63, 202 Miller-Brown Photography, Courtesy of Bandon Dunes Resort ⁓ 38, 196 Courtesy of The Boulders Resort ⁓ 26, 55, 131 Courtesy of Coeur d'Alene Resort ⁓ 42 Courtesy of Whistling Straits, Kohler, Wisconsin ⁓ 41, 160 Courtesy of The Princeville Resort ⁓ 30, 35, 56, 61, 168 Courtesy of Troon Golf (56, 61, 168 photographer Dick Durance) ⁓ 53, 120 Courtesy of Wild Wing Plantation, © 1997 Photographics ⁓ 85, 86, 227 Courtesy of Susan Goodman Smith ⁓ 138 Courtesy of Pelz Golf ⁓ 139 Courtesy of Butch Harmon ⁓ 152 Courtesy of Kenny Rankin ⁓ 156, 157 Courtesy of Michael Douglas and Catherine Zeta-Jones, © Eric Charbonneau, Berliner Studio ⁓ 181 Courtesy of the Par-Aide Products Company ⁓ 267 Courtesy of Callaway Golf Company ⁓ 308 Courtesy of Dennis Walters ⁓ 312 Courtesy of Ke'ano Kolepa - The Spirit of Golf